Passing your ITIL® Foundation Exam

London: TSO

Published by TSO (The Stationery Office) and available from:

Online
www.tsoshop.co.uk

Mail, Telephone, Fax & E-mail
TSO
PO Box 29, Norwich, NR3 1GN
Telephone orders/General enquiries: 0870 600 5522
Fax orders: 0870 600 5533
E-mail: customer.services@tso.co.uk
Textphone: 0870 240 3701

TSO@Blackwell and other Accredited Agents

First edition Crown copyright 2007
Second edition Crown copyright 2009
Third edition Crown copyright 2012

Fourth impression 2014

ISBN 9780113313556

Printed in the United Kingdom for The Stationery Office
Material is FSC certified and produced using ECF pulp, sourced from fully sustainable forests.
P002495311   c15   08/12

Contents

List of figures and tables

TABLES

Cabinet Office foreword

Congratulations – you have embarked on the start of your ITIL® journey. It will be interesting and rewarding if you use the knowledge you gain and apply it in the real world. Now the first step is to take your Foundation exam. Examinations are never easy; they are designed to test your knowledge of the subject and to enable you to prove this knowledge to yourself and others.

To help you in this, being well prepared is vital. Study aids are an essential element, and attending an accredited training course will also provide learning support, often with case studies and examples that can bring the ITIL framework to life.

This guide has been written for this very purpose, and over the years the content has been developed and expanded to incorporate the latest identified best practices. This publication will present the Foundation content in a simplified structure, ideal for learning and developing knowledge.

The content has been updated to bring it into line with the revised syllabus and to ensure that it reflects the current approach to exam questions.

The next step, of course, is to pass the examination. But, hopefully, the exam won't seem too daunting once you've studied this publication.

What you do after passing is down to you, but you have started the journey and the world of IT service management is open before you.

Best of luck!

Philip Hearsum
ITSM Portfolio Manager
Cabinet Office

Chief Examiner's foreword

'The whole purpose of education is to turn mirrors into windows.' Sydney J. Harris

The IT service management industry relies on ITIL as the wheel that turns service practices into service excellence. ITIL qualifications are the means to achieve knowledge of theory and how to apply ITIL within everyday contexts. Each ITIL qualification has become a sought-after credential to demonstrate the possession of the required skills and knowledge.

The ITIL Foundation qualification is where this educational journey begins, and it sets the foundation for understanding service management with basic concepts, principles and terminology.

No matter where you live and work, what language you speak or whether you choose to educate yourself or take an ITIL Foundation course, this publication should be considered an important tool to assist you in achieving the ITIL Foundation certification.

It nicely organizes the relevant ITIL Foundation topics in a logical and easy-to-absorb structure and sets them within the context of an unfolding story about Brigitte, a customer who takes a journey into the experience of service management.

The mind maps at the end of each chapter crystallize the content in a way that will help you to retain what you've read and make it useful as an examination preparation tool.

The sample examination questions are based on realistic examples that you will encounter at Foundation level and provide essential value for examination preparation.

This publication takes readers through the window of the ITIL Foundation curriculum and offers an interesting and lasting experience.

Sharon Taylor

ITIL Chief Examiner

The Official ITIL Accreditor's foreword

Best practice evolves and improves on a continual basis to benefit the thousands of organizations and practitioners implementing its principles across the world every day.

Changes in service management best practice over the past five years were consolidated in the publication of the latest edition of ITIL in July 2011; ITIL service management practices have become more streamlined, practical and usable for today's service managers and practitioners. Most significantly, the key improvements made to *ITIL Service Strategy* – the starting block at the very core of ITIL – mean that ITIL has become more approachable than ever before. As a result, those organizations and individuals setting out on their ITIL journey will have a smoother start and a clearer path ahead.

As the reader of this Foundation study aid, you have also taken the important first step on your ITIL journey and are giving yourself a fantastic starting point to generate and solidify a stable ITIL knowledge base. This guide is an excellent companion to other publications, course notes and materials provided by accredited training companies and is an extremely useful tool for candidates who choose to study independently at their own pace for their qualifications.

Whether this is the start of your service management career or a gateway to further your knowledge in more detailed, specialist areas, I wish you every success with your studies and examinations and, more importantly, your ongoing ITIL journey.

Richard Pharro

CEO, Official ITIL Accreditor
(part of the APM Group Ltd)

Acknowledgements

AUTHOR

Christian F. Nissen (CFN People)

All sample questions and answers were created by Michelle Hales (ConnectSphere)

REVIEWERS

Best Management Practice and The Stationery Office (TSO) would like to thank those who participated in the quality assurance of this publication, generously donating their time to reviewing this title, including:

Rosemary Gurney (Global Knowledge)

Lou Hunnebeck (Third Sky Inc.)

Michael Imhoff (Nielsen, IBM)

Stuart Rance (HP)

Thanks are still due to those who reviewed and contributed to previous editions of this title: Gary Case (Pink Elephant); Lise Dall Eriksen (CFN People); Thomas Fejfer (CFN People); Signe-Marie Hernes Bjerke (DNV); Majid Iqbal (design#code LLC); Shirley Lacy, (ConnectSphere); Ivor Macfarlane (IBM); Lars Zobbe Mortensen (Zobbe Consult & Zoftware); Bente Skøtt (OK Gasoline); Katsushi Yaginuma (ITpreneurs).

The ITIL qualification
scheme

1

1 The ITIL qualification scheme

ITIL (formerly known as the IT Infrastructure Library) is best practice for IT service management, which is used by many organizations around the world. A whole ITIL philosophy has grown up around the advice contained within the ITIL publications and the supporting certification and qualification scheme.

The purpose of the ITIL qualification scheme is to ensure that relevant and timely certifications are available to support the formalized learning requirements of individuals and organizations related to the ITIL service management practices.

The official ITIL qualification scheme is the only training and qualification scheme leading to official ITIL qualifications in IT service management.

1.1 LEVELS OF QUALIFICATION

The ITIL qualificat ion scheme introduces a learning system that enables an individual to gain credits for all ITIL courses that can be applied towards a recognized professional achievement (see Figure 1.1). Once candidates have accumulated a sufficient number of credits, they can be awarded the ITIL Expert in IT service management certification.

To achieve ITIL Expert certification, candidates must obtain a minimum of 22 credits, 2 of which must be from the Foundation module, which is a mandatory first step, and 5 of which must be from the 'Managing Across the Lifecycle' module, which is the mandatory final step.

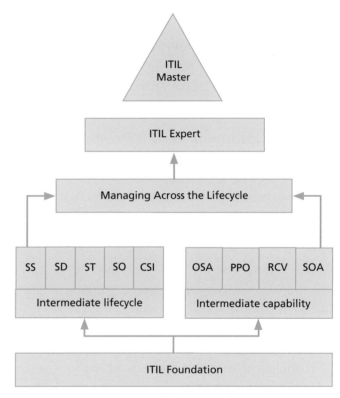

Figure 1.1 The ITIL qualification scheme

Candidates can choose modules from the Service Capability (4 credits per module) or Service Lifecycle (3 credits per module) streams to gain the other 15 credits, but are expected to choose a balanced programme overall.

1.1.1 ITIL Foundation certificate in IT service management

The Foundation level is the entry-level qualification, which offers candidates a general awareness of the key elements, concepts and terminology used in the ITIL service lifecycle, including the linkages between lifecycle stages, the processes used and their contribution to service management practices.

More details of the ITIL Foundation certificate in IT service management can be found in section 1.3.

1.1.2 ITIL Intermediate qualification certificates in IT service management

ITIL Intermediate level has a modular structure, with each module holding a different focus. Candidates can take as few or as many Intermediate qualifications as they require, and to suit their needs. The Intermediate modules go into more detail than the Foundation level.

The Intermediate qualifications are grouped in two sets:

■ The **Service Lifecycle Stream**, which will be of interest to candidates seeking a management/ team leader role that requires a broad management focus of ITIL practice areas and work across teams or multiple-capability areas. The prime focus is the lifecycle itself, the use of process and practice elements within it, and the management capabilities needed to deliver quality service management practices in an organization. An examination is taken for each module.

■ The **Service Capability Stream**, which will be of interest to candidates who wish to gain intense, specialized, process-level knowledge in one or more processes, with focus on the day-to-day execution of ITIL practices. Attention to the service lifecycle is illustrated as part of the curriculum; however, the primary focus is on the process activities, execution and use throughout the service lifecycle. An examination is taken for each module.

Both Intermediate streams assess an individual's comprehension and application of the concepts of ITIL. Candidates are able to take units from either of the Intermediate streams or may combine units from both streams. These units give them credits towards an ITIL Expert certificate.

1.1.2.1 Service Lifecycle

The Intermediate Service Lifecycle Stream is built around the five ITIL core publications:

■ *ITIL Service Strategy* (SS)
■ *ITIL Service Design* (SD)
■ *ITIL Service Transition* (ST)
■ *ITIL Service Operation* (SO)
■ *ITIL Continual Service Improvement* (CSI).

1.1.2.2 Service Capability

The Intermediate Service Capability Stream is built around four clusters:

■ Operational support and analysis (OSA)
■ Service offerings and agreements (SOA)
■ Planning, protection and optimization (PPO)
■ Release, control and validation (RCV).

1.1.3 Managing Across the Lifecycle (MALC)

The ITIL Managing Across the Lifecycle (MALC) qualification is a capstone qualification, focusing on the knowledge required to implement and manage the necessary skills associated with use of the lifecycle practices. It is the final required module which a candidate must take prior to achieving ITIL Expert level.

1.1.4 ITIL Expert in IT service management certificate

The ITIL Expert level of qualification is aimed at those individuals who are interested in demonstrating a superior level of knowledge of the ITIL scheme in its entirety.

Once a candidate has successfully completed all requisite ITIL modules and has earned sufficient credits, they will be awarded the ITIL Expert in IT service management certificate. No further examination or course is required to gain the ITIL Expert certificate.

1.1.5 ITIL Master in IT service management certificate

The ITIL Master in IT service management certificate validates the capability of the candidate to apply the principles, methods and techniques of ITIL in the workplace.

To achieve the ITIL Master qualification the candidate must be able to explain and justify how they selected and individually applied a range of knowledge, principles, methods and techniques from ITIL and supporting management techniques, to achieve desired business outcomes in one or more practical assignments.

To be eligible for the ITIL Master qualification, candidates must meet or fulfil the following entry criteria:

- Have reached the ITIL Expert level
- Have worked in IT service management for at least five years in leadership, managerial or higher management advisory levels.

Details of the various learning options, certifications and combinations can be found on the ITIL qualification scheme website: www.itil-officialsite. com/Qualifications/ITILQualificationScheme.aspx

1.2 QUALIFICATIONS BODIES

This section outlines the roles of the organizations within the official ITIL qualification scheme. Candidates should ensure that when buying ITIL training, it is acquired from an ITIL-accredited organization.

1.2.1 Cabinet Office

ITIL was originally developed by the UK government organization Central Computer and Telecommunications Agency (CCTA), which in 2000 was merged into the Office of Government Commerce (OGC), an office of HM Treasury. In 2010 OGC was moved into the Cabinet Office, which is now the owner of ITIL and several other best-practice products.

The Cabinet Office has established collaborative partnerships with two organizations to provide support for its ITIL portfolio. As the official accreditor, the APM Group provides accreditation services related to examination institutes and training providers, and is responsible for the qualification scheme. The Stationery Office (TSO) is the official publisher of all official ITIL library publications, including this one.

The Cabinet Office retains the rights to all intellectual property, copyright and trademarks relating to ITIL. Its predominant role in the official scheme is one of ownership and stewardship of the ITIL library content and qualifications. The APM Group chairs the qualifications board (the steering committee made up of representatives from the community who make decisions about qualifications policy) and ensures that decisions made are to the benefit of ITIL and users alike.

1.2.2 APM Group

The APM Group is an international professional accreditation and certification body, which is accredited to international standards by the United Kingdom Accreditation Service (UKAS), which ensures the effectiveness, impartiality and quality of APM Group scheme administration services. In 2006, the APM Group became the Cabinet Office's official accreditor for ITIL and is now responsible for the monitoring and promotion of the official scheme for training, consulting and qualifications.

Within its role as the official ITIL accreditor, the APM Group is responsible for setting the standards and syllabuses throughout the market, which any delivering examination institute must adhere to, as well as creating, maintaining and delivering the ITIL qualification scheme itself.

The APM Group is also responsible for the accreditation and monitoring of any examination institute applying to the official scheme to run ITIL qualifications and accredit training organizations.

1.2.3 Examination institutes

The APM Group as the official accreditor is authorized to license other examination institutes to administer ITIL qualifications and accreditation activities. Under the contracts signed with the APM Group, examination institutes are allowed to conduct the following activities:

- Approve training organizations
- Administer examinations via those organizations that they have approved.

The list of the current examination institutes can be found at www.itil-officialsite.com/ ExaminationInstitutes/ExamInstitutes.aspx

1.2.4 Accredited training organizations

Accredited training organizations (ATOs), sometimes known as accredited course providers (ACPs), are companies that have been assessed and approved by an examination institute to run officially accredited training courses and administer examinations in ITIL.

These accredited organizations must submit:

- Their quality management systems, detailing their processes for administration of the training courses and examinations
- The course material they use to train ITIL candidates for the examinations
- Their trainers for assessment by an examination institute.

Following approval by an examination institute, ATOs are granted a licence by the APM Group as the official accreditor to use the relevant Cabinet Office-owned intellectual property rights and trademarks relating to ITIL. A list of current accredited training organizations can be found at www.itil-officialsite.com/ TrainingOrganisations/ATOListing.aspx

1.2.5 *it*SMF International

The IT Service Management Forum (*it*SMF) is the not-for-profit international community for IT service management professionals, with more than 50 chapters worldwide and a coordinating organization – *it*SMF International (www.itsmfi.org). The chapters provide local support to those individuals and organizations using and implementing ITIL.

*it*SMF is recognized as an integral part of the ITIL community. It is a collaborative partner to the ITIL official scheme and participates on the qualifications board.

1.3   THE ITIL FOUNDATION CERTIFICATE IN IT SERVICE MANAGEMENT

1.3.1 Purpose

The purpose of the ITIL Foundation certificate in IT service management is to certify that the candidate has gained knowledge of the ITIL terminology, structure and basic concepts and has comprehended the core principles of ITIL practices for service management.

The ITIL Foundation certificate in IT service management is *not* intended to enable the holders of the certificate to *apply* the ITIL practices for service management without further guidance.

1.3.2 Target group

The target group of the ITIL Foundation certificate in IT service management is drawn from:

■ Individuals who require a basic understanding of the ITIL framework and how it may be used to enhance the quality of IT service management within an organization

■ IT professionals who are working within an organization that has adopted and adapted ITIL, who need to be informed about and thereafter contribute to an ongoing service improvement programme.

1.3.3 Prerequisites

There are no formal criteria or prerequisites for candidates wishing to attend an accredited ITIL Foundation course, though some familiarity with IT terminology and an appreciation of their own business environment is recommended.

Accredited ITIL Foundation training is strongly recommended but is not a prerequisite.

1.3.4 Learning objectives

The learning objectives of the ITIL Foundation certification in IT service management are to enable the candidate to:

■ Define the concept of a service and to comprehend and explain the concept of service management as a practice.

■ Understand the value of the ITIL service lifecycle, how the processes integrate with each other throughout the lifecycle, and explain the objectives, scope and business value for each phase in the lifecycle.

■ Define some of the key terminology and explain the key concepts of service management.

■ Comprehend and account for the key principles and models of service management, and balance some of the opposing forces within service management.

■ Understand how the service management processes contribute to the ITIL service lifecycle, to explain the purpose, objectives, scope, basic concepts, activities and interfaces for four of the core processes, and state the purpose, objectives and scope for 18 of the remaining processes.

- Explain the role, objectives and organizational structures of the service desk function, and state the role and objectives of three other functions.
- Account for and be aware of the responsibilities of some of the key roles in service management.
- Understand how service automation assists with expediting service management processes.
- Be aware of the role of competence and training for service management and explain the ITIL qualification scheme.

1.3.5 Reference

The full syllabus with detailed descriptions of each of the learning objectives can be downloaded from the ITIL website: www.itil-officialsite.com/Qualifications/ITILQualificationLevels/ITILFoundation.aspx

1.4 ABOUT THIS PUBLICATION

This publication is based on the syllabus for the ITIL Foundation certificate in IT service management. It is therefore neither an introduction to ITIL nor a brief summary of the ITIL core publications. Rather, it is a study aid to support the adoption of knowledge and skills required to achieve the ITIL Foundation certificate in IT service management.

One of the Foundation learning objectives is to understand the common terminology used within ITIL, and readers may find it useful to access the official ITIL glossary of terms and definitions (see www.best-management-practice. com and navigate to 'Glossaries and Acronyms').

The structure of this publication does not strictly follow the order of the syllabus. Instead it is structured with ease of learning in mind. Basic concepts are introduced in Chapters 2 and 3 ('Introduction to service management' and 'ITIL and the service lifecycle') to provide the basis for the concepts, principles and practices that are introduced in the subsequent five chapters, each representing a core publication. Each of the five core chapters is identically structured to help the acquisition of the covered concepts, principles and practices. The two subsequent chapters ('Service management technology' and 'How it all fits together') contain topics that span the five core publications.

At the end of Chapters 2 to 9, a mind map and a number of sample test questions are presented to enable the reader to rehearse and practise the content of the chapter. The number of questions in each chapter corresponds to the typical distribution of questions in an exam.

It is hoped that you will find service management enjoyable and you will acquire the new knowledge and skills necessary for achieving the ITIL Foundation certificate in IT service management.

Introduction to
service management

2 Introduction to service management

'People do not want quarter-inch drills. They want quarter-inch holes.' Professor Emeritus Theodore Levitt, Harvard Business School

2.1 SERVICES AND SERVICE MANAGEMENT

2.1.1 Services

Case study: service management in practice (Brigitte's experience)

Brigitte enters an alpine hotel in a medium-sized town in Switzerland. She is on a short business trip and needs to stay over for the next two nights. She has just got out of the taxi and approaches the hotel reception to ask for a service from the hotel: accommodation.

To understand what service management is, we need first to understand what services are, and how service management can help service providers to deliver and manage these services. First of all, *services are a means of delivering value to customers by facilitating the outcomes customers want to achieve*.

Definition

Outcome is the result of carrying out an activity, following a process, delivering an IT service etc. The term is used to refer to the *intended* results, as well as to *actual* results.

The outcomes that customers want to achieve are the reason why they purchase or use a service. The value of the service to the customer is directly dependent on how well a service facilitates these outcomes.

Definitions

A **service** is a means of delivering value to customers by facilitating the outcomes customers want to achieve without the ownership of specific costs and risks.

An **IT service** is a service provided by an IT service provider. An IT service is made up of a combination of information technology, people and processes.

If you buy an apartment, the ownership of the specific costs and risks are transferred to you as part of the deal. But if you stay at a hotel, the ownership of the specific costs and risks remains with the service provider. The same is the case if you take a taxi instead of driving your own car.

Case study: service management in practice (Brigitte's experience)

Brigitte has never thought of it in that way. She is going to inspect the production of a medical company tomorrow; the overnight accommodation enables her to start work very early in the morning and it reduces the geographical constraints put on her by living in Denmark.

Brigitte gets a room that satisfies her need to stay overnight without having to undertake the cost and risk of owning her own apartment in Switzerland.

2.1.2 Service types

IT services that are seen by the customer are called customer-facing services. These are typically services that support the customer's business processes, directly facilitating some outcomes desired by the customer.

Just as there are internal and external customers, there are internal and external customer-facing services. Internal customer-facing services are delivered between departments or business units in the same organization. External customer-facing services are delivered to external customers.

The reason for differentiating between internal and external customer-facing services is to distinguish between services that support an internal business activity and those that actually achieve business outcomes. The difference may not appear to be significant at first, since the activity to deliver the services is often similar. However, it is important to recognize that internal services have to be linked to external services before their contribution to business outcomes can be understood and measured.

Customer-facing services are normally enabled by supporting services that are required by the service provider to underpin the customer-facing services. These are typically invisible to the customer, but essential to the delivery of customer-facing services. Supporting services may be of many different types or go by a variety of names, such as infrastructure services, network services, application services or technical services.

> **Definitions**
>
> An **internal customer-facing service** is an IT service that directly supports a business process managed by another business unit – for example, a sales-reporting service or enterprise resource management.
>
> An **external customer-facing service** is an IT service that is directly provided to an external customer – for example, internet access at an airport.
>
> A **supporting service** is an IT service that is not directly used by the business but is required by the IT service provider to deliver customer-facing services (for example, a directory service or a backup service). Supporting services may also include IT services only used by the IT service provider.

Figure 2.1 shows the difference between internal and external customer-facing services and supporting services for an IT service provider.

2.1.3 Core, enabling and enhancing services

All services, whether internal, external or supporting, can be further classified in terms of how they relate to one another and their customers:

- **Core services** deliver the basic outcomes desired by the customer. They represent the value that the customer wants and for which they are willing to pay.
- **Enabling services** are services that are needed in order to deliver a core service. Enabling services may or may not be visible to the customer, but they are not offered to customers in their own right.

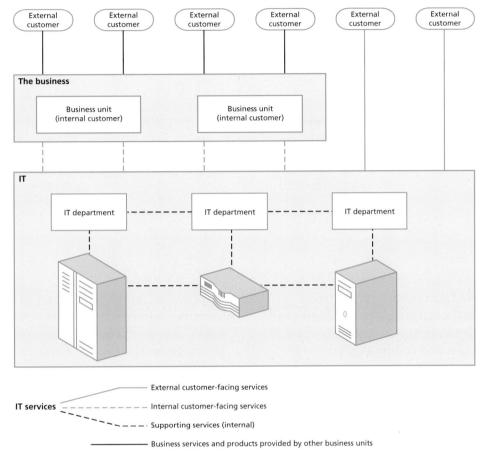

Figure 2.1 Internal, external and supporting services

■ **Enhancing services** are services that are added to a core service to make it more attractive to the customer. Enhancing services are not essential to the delivery of a core service but are used to encourage customers to use the core services or to differentiate the service provider from its competitors.

Examples of the service types are provided in Table 2.1.

2.1.4 Service packaging

Most service providers will follow a strategy of delivering a set of more generic services to a broad range of customers, thus achieving economies of scale. One way of achieving this flexibility is by using service packages.

Table 2.1 Examples of core, enabling and enhancing services

	Core service	Enabling service	Enhancing service
IT services (office automation)	Word processing	Download and installation of updates	Document publication to professional printer for high-quality brochure
IT services (benefits tracking)	Employees of a company can monitor the status of their benefits (such as health insurance and retirement accounts).	A portal that provides a user-friendly front-end access to the benefits-tracking service.	Customers can create and manage a fitness or weight-loss programme. Customers who show progress in their programme are awarded a discount on their premiums.

Definition

A **service package** is a collection of two or more services that have been combined to offer a solution to a specific type of customer need or to underpin specific business outcomes. A service package can consist of a combination of core services, enabling services, enhancing services and other service packages.

Where a service or service package needs to be differentiated for various types of customer, one or more components of the package can be changed, or offered at different service levels, to create service options. These different service options can then be offered to customers and are sometimes called *service level packages*.

Some supporting services such as service desk, typically bundled with most service packages, can also be offered on their own (see Figure 2.2).

Case study: service management in practice (Brigitte's experience)

Brigitte realizes that she is part of a very specific customer segment. She is not travelling with her family as a tourist but is recognized by the hotel as a business customer. On the other hand she is probably not considered a VIP by the hotel. The hotel has carefully designed a service package for her segment with room, breakfast, wireless broadband connection, parking and internet booking. It offers different service options for her segment as well.

When she booked the hotel, Brigitte had the opportunity to select an ordinary room instead of the suite she chose. The hotel even offered an add-on service option with the possibility of cancellation until the day of arrival.

2.1.5 Service value: utility and warranty

The value of a service can be considered to be the level to which that service meets a customer's expectations. Unlike products, services do not have much intrinsic value. The value of a service comes

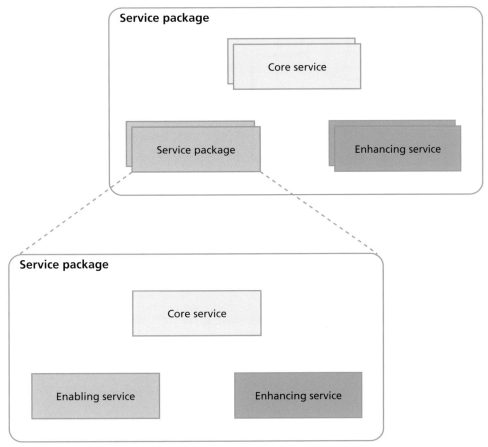

Figure 2.2 Service packages can contain other service packages

from what it enables someone to do. A service contributes value to an organization only when its value is perceived to be higher than the cost of obtaining the service.

From the customer's perspective, value consists of achieving business objectives. The value of a service is created by combining two primary elements (see Figure 2.3):

- **Utility** What the customer gets – or fitness for purpose
- **Warranty** How it is delivered – or fitness for use.

Definition

Utility is the functionality offered by a product or service to meet a particular need.

Utility can be summarized as 'what the service does', and can be used to determine whether a service is able to meet its required outcomes, or is 'fit for

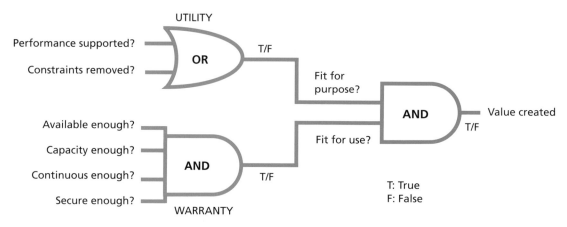

Figure 2.3 Value is created from service utilities and warranties

purpose'. Utility increases the average performance of customers' assets by improving customers' productivity or outcomes or by removing constraints on their performance.

> **Definition**
>
> **Warranty** is the assurance that a product or service will meet its agreed requirements. This may be a formal agreement such as a service level agreement or contract, or it may be a marketing message or brand image.

Warranty refers to the ability of a service to be *available* when needed, to provide the required *capacity*, and to provide the required reliability in terms of *continuity* and *security*. Warranty can be summarized as 'how the service is delivered', and can be used to determine whether a service is 'fit for use'.

Warranty decreases the possible losses for the customer from variation in performance. Customers feel more certain that their demand for service will be fulfilled with the same level of utility with little variation.

It should be noted that the elements of warranty in Figure 2.3 (availability, capacity, continuity and security) are not exclusive. It is possible to define other components of warranty, such as usability or compliance.

> **Case study: service management in practice (Brigitte's experience)**
>
> It is the first time Brigitte has been confronted with the concept of utility and warranty, but when she thinks about it, it makes perfect sense.
>
> She looks around. The bed, table and bathroom are good examples of utility in that they fulfil her need for sleep, the ability to work in her room and to have a bath before she leaves for her appointment tomorrow.
>
> But to create value, the room must be available on the night she needs it, there must be internet bandwidth enough for her to prepare for the next day's work on her laptop, and she must feel secure in her room. These conditions are examples of warranty.

Customers cannot benefit from something that is fit for purpose but not fit for use, and vice versa. The value of a service is therefore only delivered when both utility and warranty are designed and delivered.

2.1.6 Service assets: resources and capabilities

To create value in the form of goods and services, an organization needs assets. A service asset is any resource or capability used by a service provider to deliver services to a customer (see Table 2.2 for examples).

Definition

Resource is a generic term, which includes IT infrastructure, people, money or anything else that might help to deliver an IT service. Resources are considered to be assets of an organization.

Case study: service management in practice (Brigitte's experience)

Brigitte takes a quick walk around the hotel. Despite its small size, the hotel possesses quite a lot of resources. These include a well-equipped and cosy dining room, a wine cellar, hotel staff, bathrooms, information brochures and place to park her car.

However, Brigitte can't help thinking that the resources would be of no use if it were not for capabilities such as the attitude, skills, knowledge and experience of the staff, their way of organizing the hotel, and a number of well-practised processes that cannot be taken for granted.

Resources are direct inputs for production.

Capabilities on the other hand represent an organization's ability to coordinate, control and deploy resources to produce value. Capabilities such as management, organization, people and knowledge are used to transform resources into valuable services.

Definition

Capability is the ability of a service organization, person, process, application, IT service or other configuration item to carry out an activity. Capabilities are intangible assets of an organization.

Capabilities are typically experience-driven, knowledge-intensive, information-based and firmly embedded within an organization's people, systems, processes and technologies.

It is relatively easy to acquire resources in comparison with capabilities. Typically, distinctive capabilities can only be developed over time and are hard for competitors to duplicate.

The distinctive capabilities of a service provider set it apart from its competitors and enable it to attract and retain customers by offering unique value propositions.

Table 2.2 Examples of capabilities and resources

Capabilities	Resources
Management	Financial capital
Organization	Infrastructure
Processes	Applications
Knowledge	Information
People (experience, skills and relationships)	People (number of employees)

2.1.7 Service composition

Case study: service management in practice (Brigitte's experience)

A service such as accommodation for one night, which at a first glance looks very simple, seems to be much more complicated behind the scenes. The hotel needs to know Brigitte's 'business process'. Staff need to catalogue their services to help Brigitte select the right service for her needs; they need to sign an agreement with Brigitte to establish and maintain the appropriate infrastructure at the hotel, to secure and operate the environment, and to gather and maintain data not only about Brigitte but also on all other aspects of the service such as money, food, facilities and so on.

The hotel needs to provide an internet application and to acquire supporting services such as wireless access, laundry, newspapers and so on.

The hotel also needs to set up agreements internally with its staff and externally with its suppliers to clarify responsibilities and levels of quality, and continually train and measure all parties to ensure a high and consistent standard.

In summary, the composition of a service and its constituent parts can now be defined as illustrated in Figure 2.4.

All the components of the service and their interrelationships have to be considered, ensuring that the services delivered meet new and evolving business needs. The various components are:

- **Business process** The process that defines the functional needs of the service being provided, e.g. telesales, invoicing, orders, credit checking

- **Service** The service itself that is being delivered to customers and business by the service provider, e.g. email and billing

- **Service design package (SDP)** Document(s) defining all aspects of a service and its requirements through each stage of its lifecycle

- **Business case** Justification for service investments and expenditure

- **Service level agreements (SLAs)/service level requirements (SLRs)** Documents agreed with the customer that specify the level, scope and quality of service to be provided

- **Infrastructure** All of the IT equipment necessary to deliver the service to customers and users, including servers, network circuits, switches, personal computers (PCs) and telephones

- **Environment** The environment required to secure and operate the infrastructure, e.g. data centres, power and air conditioning

- **Data** The data necessary to support the service and provide the information required by the business processes, e.g. customer records and accounts ledger

- **Applications** All of the software applications required to manipulate the data and provide the functional requirements of the business processes, e.g. enterprise resource management (ERM), financial and customer relationship management (CRM)

- **Integration** Solutions to combine applications or data from different sources and providing a user or an application with a unified view of these applications and data

- **Operational level agreements (OLAs) and contracts** Any underpinning agreements necessary to deliver the quality of service agreed within a service level agreement (SLA)

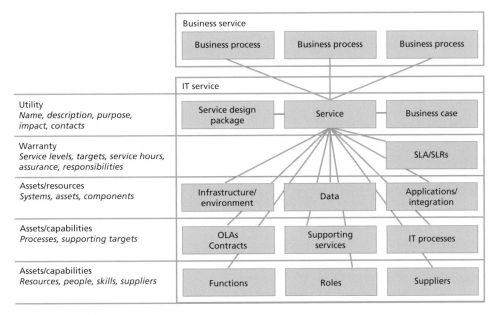

Figure 2.4 Service composition

- **Supporting services** Any services that are necessary to support the operation of the delivered service, e.g. a shared service or a managed network service
- **IT processes** The processes needed by the service provider to ensure successful provision of the service, e.g. request fulfilment, incident management, change management and availability management
- **Functions** Any internal teams providing support for any of the components required to provide the service, e.g. the service desk
- **Roles** Responsibilities, activities and authorities granted to a person or team that control and deploy the resources engaged in the service, e.g. problem manager, release manager, capacity manager and service owner

- **Suppliers** External third parties necessary to provide support for any of the components required to provide the service, e.g. networks, hardware, software.

2.1.8 Service management

Service management is what enables a service provider to understand the services they are providing; to ensure that the services really do facilitate the outcomes their customers want to achieve; to understand the value of the services to their customers; and to understand and manage all the costs and risks associated with those services.

Definitions

Service management is a set of specialized organizational capabilities for providing value to customers in the form of services.

IT service management (ITSM) is the implementation and management of quality IT services that meet the needs of the business. IT service management is performed by IT service providers through an appropriate mix of people, process and information technology.

These capabilities include the management practices, processes, functions, roles, knowledge and skills that a service provider uses to enable them to deliver services that create value to their customers. The capabilities represent their capacity, competency and confidence for action. The more mature a service provider's capabilities are, the greater is their ability to consistently produce quality services that meet the needs of the customer in a timely and cost-effective manner.

The act of transforming resources (Figure 2.5) into valuable services by exploiting the organization's capabilities is at the core of service management. Without the capabilities, a service organization is merely a bundle of useless resources.

However, service management is more than just a set of capabilities. It is also a professional practice supported by an extensive body of knowledge, experience and skills. A global community of individuals and organizations fosters its growth and maturity.

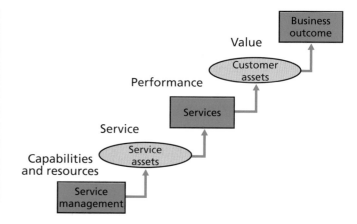

Figure 2.5 Service management is the act of transforming resources into valuable services

Case study: service management in practice (Brigitte's experience)

As a service provider the hotel needs to establish functions such as a concierge, reception, kitchen and facilities management as well as processes such as booking, request fulfilment, capacity management and cooking. They are all examples of capabilities that help the hotel to transform resources in the form of staff, food and buildings into valuable hotel services.

But the hotel must also ensure that it hires people who have acquired the appropriate level of knowledge and skills through education and experience within the profession.

2.1.9 Stakeholders in service management

Stakeholders have an interest in an organization, project, service etc. and may be interested in the activities, targets, resources or deliverables from service management. Examples of stakeholders include organizations, service providers, customers, consumers, users, partners, employees, shareholders, owners and suppliers.

2.1.9.1 Service providers

Every IT organization should act as a service provider, using the principles of service management to ensure that they deliver the outcomes required by their customers.

> **Definition**
>
> A **service provider** is an organization supplying services to one or more internal customers or external customers.

It is necessary to distinguish between different types of service provider. There are three main types of service provider:

- **Type I – internal service provider** An internal service provider that is embedded within a business unit. There may be several Type I service providers within an organization.
- **Type II – shared services unit** An internal service provider that provides shared IT services to more than one business unit.
- **Type III – external service provider** A service provider that provides IT services to external customers.

In reality most organizations have a combination of the three types of IT service providers.

2.1.9.2 Customers

> **Definition**
>
> A **customer** is someone who buys goods or services. The customer of an IT service provider is the person or group who defines and agrees the service level targets.

There is a difference between customers who work in the same organization as the IT service provider and customers who work for other organizations. They are distinguished as follows:

- **Internal customers** These are customers who work for the same business as the IT service provider. For example, the marketing department is an internal customer of the IT organization because it uses IT services. The head of marketing and the chief information officer both report to the chief executive officer. If IT charges for its services, the money paid is an internal transaction in the organization's accounting system, not real revenue.
- **External customers** These are customers who work for a different business from the IT service provider. External customers typically purchase services from the service provider by means of a legally binding contract or agreement.

It is important to note that both internal and external customers must be provided with the agreed level of service. The way in which services are designed, transitioned, delivered and improved, however, is often quite different. Examples are funding, links to business strategy and objectives, accounting, involvement in service design, transition and operation as well as drivers for improvement.

2.1.9.3 Users

While customers actually pay for and negotiate the level of services with the service provider, they usually do so on behalf of a number of users or consumers.

> **Definition**
>
> A **user** is a person who uses the service on a day-to-day basis. Users are distinct from customers, as some customers do not use the IT service directly.

It is critical for the service provider to actively engage with these users to ensure that the services meet the needs of both customers and users.

2.1.9.4 Suppliers

> **Definition**
>
> A **supplier** is a third party responsible for supplying goods or services that are required to deliver services.

Examples of suppliers include commodity hardware and software vendors, network and telecom providers, and outsourcing organizations.

2.2 PROCESSES, FUNCTIONS AND ROLES

Processes, functions and roles are key service management capabilities of an organization.

2.2.1 Processes

> **Definition**
>
> A **process** is a structured set of activities designed to accomplish a specific objective. A process takes one or more defined inputs and turns them into defined outputs.

Processes define actions, dependencies and sequence. Well-defined processes can improve productivity within and across organizations and functions. It may include any of the roles, responsibilities, tools and management controls required to reliably deliver the outputs. A process may define policies, standards, guidelines, activities and work instructions if they are needed.

> **Case study: service management in practice (Brigitte's experience)**
>
> Brigitte has been at this hotel on a number of occasions, so she recognizes the various processes, which include booking, check-in, cleaning, fulfilling reasonable needs of the guests, managing errors and complaints, ensuring adequate capacity, managing finances, issuing invoices, providing meals and other refreshments, dealing with changes or new demands, maintaining buildings and equipment, and checkout.

2.2.1.1 Process model

Processes, once defined, should be documented and controlled. Once under control, they can be repeated and managed. Process measurement and metrics can be built into the process to control and improve the process, as illustrated in Figure 2.6.

The process model shows that data enters the process, is processed, is output, and the outcome is measured and reviewed.

A process is organized around a set of objectives. The main outputs from the process should be driven by the objectives and should include process measurements (metrics), reports and process improvement. A process should be owned

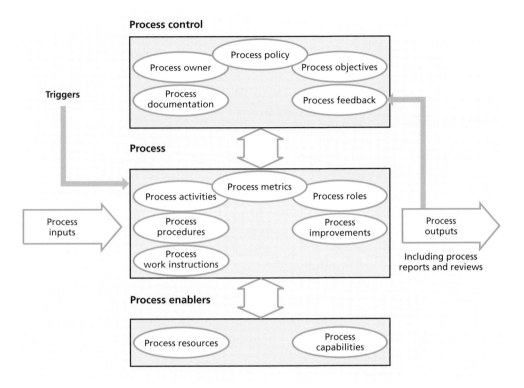

Figure 2.6 Process model

by a process owner, who should be accountable for the process and its improvement and for ensuring that the process meets its objectives.

The output produced by a process has to conform to operational norms that are derived from business objectives. If products conform to the set norm, the process can be considered effective (because it can be repeated, measured and managed). If the activities are carried out with a minimum use of resources, the process can also be considered efficient.

Inputs are data or information used by the process and may be the output from another process.

A process, or an activity within a process, is initiated by a trigger. A trigger may be the arrival of an input or other event. For example, the failure of a server may trigger the event management and incident management processes.

A process may include any of the roles, responsibilities, tools and management controls required to reliably deliver the outputs. A process may define policies, standards, guidelines, activities and work instructions if they are needed.

Process analysis, results and metrics should be incorporated in regular management reports and process improvements.

Documentation standards, processes and templates should be used to ensure that the processes are easily adopted throughout an organization.

2.2.1.2 Process characteristics

Process characteristics include:

- **Measurability** Ability to measure the process in a relevant manner. This is performance-driven. Managers want to measure cost, quality and other variables while practitioners are concerned with duration and productivity.
- **Specific results** The reason a process exists is to deliver a specific result. This result must be individually identifiable and countable.
- **Customers** Every process delivers its primary results to a customer or stakeholder. Customers may be internal or external to the organization, but the process must meet their expectations.
- **Responsiveness to specific triggers** While a process may be ongoing or iterative, it should be traceable to a specific trigger.

2.2.2 Functions

Case study: service management in practice (Brigitte's experience)

Brigitte sits down at the desk in order to go over a few things before the meeting next day, only to realize that the bulb in the lamp on the table has failed. Brigitte calls the reception. The issue is easily solved because the reception acts as a single point of contact to the other functions at the hotel. Soon a staff member from the facilities function knocks on her door and exchanges the bulb.

Definition

A **function** is a team or group of people and the tools or other resources they use to carry out one or more processes or activities – for example, the service desk.

In larger organizations, a function may be broken out and performed by several departments, teams and groups, or it may be embodied within a single organizational unit. In smaller organizations, one person or group can perform multiple functions.

Functions tend to optimize work methods locally to focus on assigned outcomes. Poor coordination between functions combined with an inward focus leads to functional silos that hinder cross-organizational cooperation. Appropriate organizational structure of teams, groups or functions therefore needs to be established and managed.

2.2.3 Roles

Delivering service successfully depends on personnel involved in service management having the appropriate education, training, skills and experience. People need to understand their role and how they contribute to the overall organization, services and processes to be effective and motivated. As changes are made, job requirements, roles, responsibilities and competencies should be updated if necessary.

Definition

A **role** is a set of responsibilities, activities and authorities assigned to a person or team. A role is defined in a process or function.

The specific roles within service management all require specific skills, attributes and competences from the people involved to enable them to work effectively and efficiently. However, whatever the role, it is imperative that the person carrying out that role has the following attributes:

■ Awareness of the business priorities, business objectives and business drivers
■ Awareness of the role IT plays in enabling the business objectives to be met
■ Customer service skills
■ Awareness of what IT can deliver to the business, including capabilities
■ The competence, knowledge and information necessary to complete the role
■ The ability to use, understand and interpret the best practice, policies and procedures to ensure adherence.

The following are examples of attributes required in many of the roles, dependent on the organization and the specific roles assigned:

■ Management skills – both from a people management perspective and from the overall control of process.
■ Ability to handle meetings – organizing, chairing, and documenting meetings and ensuring that actions are followed up.
■ Communication skills – an important element of all roles is raising awareness of the processes in place to ensure buy-in and conformance. An ability to communicate at all levels within the organization will be imperative.
■ Articulateness – both written (e.g. for reports) and oral.
■ Negotiation skills for several aspects, such as procurement and contracts.
■ An analytical mind – to analyse metrics produced from the activity.

For service management to be successful, an organization will need to clearly define the specific roles and responsibilities required to undertake the processes and activities involved in each lifecycle stage. These roles will need to be assigned to individuals.

Case study: service management in practice (Brigitte's experience)

At the small hotel where Brigitte is staying, only a few roles are necessary to manage the delivery of services. In a larger hotel or a hotel chain, a greater number of other roles might be needed, such as:

■ Account manager
■ Contract manager
■ Security manager
■ Purchasing manager
■ Project director
■ Reception manager.

One person or team may have multiple roles, for example the roles of configuration manager and change manager may be carried out by a single person. On the other hand, one role is often carried out by multiple people: the problem analyst role may for example be assigned to more than one person. In a hotel scenario, a waiter might work as a dishwasher when the guests have left the restaurant. A small hotel might have just one employee undertaking the two roles, whereas a large hotel is more likely to have only one role per employee.

Roles fall into two main categories – generic roles such as process manager and process owner, and specific roles that are involved within a particular lifecycle stage or process such as an incident manager or IT designer/architect.

2.2.3.1 RACI

When designing a service or a process, it is imperative that all the roles are clearly defined. Since services, processes and their activities run through an entire organization, the individual activities should be clearly mapped to well-defined roles. A RACI authority matrix (see Table 2.3) is often used within organizations to define the roles and responsibilities in relation to processes and activities. RACI is an acronym for the four main roles of being:

- **Responsible** The person or people responsible for getting the job done.
- **Accountable** The person who has ownership of quality and the end result. Only one person can be accountable for each task.
- **Consulted** The people who are consulted and whose opinions are sought.
- **Informed** The people who are kept up to date on progress.

The RACI chart shows the structure of RACI modelling. The rows represent a number of required activities and the columns identify the people who make the decisions, carry out activities or provide input.

ITIL defines numerous roles. Four of the generic roles are outlined below.

2.2.3.2 Service owner

The service owner is accountable for a specific service within an organization, regardless of where the underpinning technology components, processes or professional capabilities reside.

Service ownership is as critical to service management as establishing ownership for processes, which crosses multiple vertical silos or departments.

The service owner's accountabilities include:

- Representing the service across the organization
- Understanding the service
- Working with business relationship management to understand and translate customer requirements into activities, measures or service components that will ensure that the service provider can meet those requirements
- Ensuring consistent and appropriate communication with customers for service-related enquiries and issues
- Ensuring that the ongoing service delivery and support meet agreed customer requirements

Table 2.3 An example of a simple RACI matrix

	Director of service management	Service level manager	Problem manager	Security manager	Procurement manager
Activity 1	AR	C	I	I	C
Activity 2	AR	R	C	C	C
Activity 3	I	A	R	I	C
Activity 4	I	A	R	I	
Activity 5	I	R	A	C	I

- Participating in negotiating service level agreements (SLAs) and operating level agreements (OLAs)
- Representing the service in change advisory board (CAB) meetings
- Liaising with the appropriate process owners throughout the service lifecycle
- Participating in internal service review meetings within IT and external service review meetings with the business
- Identifying and making improvements to the service
- Being accountable for the delivery of the service.

2.2.3.3 Process owner

The process owner role is accountable for ensuring that a process is fit for purpose. This role is often assigned to the same person who carries out the process manager role, but the two roles may be separate in larger organizations. The process owner role is accountable for ensuring that their process is performed according to the agreed and documented standard and meets the aims of the process definition.

The process owner's accountabilities include:

- Sponsoring, designing and change managing the process and its metrics
- Defining, evaluating and maintaining the process strategy
- Assisting with process design
- Ensuring that appropriate process documentation is available and current
- Defining appropriate policies and standards to be employed throughout the process
- Periodically auditing the process to ensure compliance with policy and standards

- Communicating process information or changes as appropriate to ensure awareness
- Providing process resources to support activities required throughout the service lifecycle
- Ensuring that process technicians have the required knowledge and the required technical and business understanding to deliver the process, and understand their role in the process
- Addressing issues with the running of the process
- Identifying process improvement opportunities
- Making improvements to the process.

2.2.3.4 Process manager

The process manager role is accountable for operational management of a process. There may be several process managers for one process, for example regional change managers or IT service continuity managers for each data centre. The process manager role is often assigned to the person who carries out the process owner role, but the two roles may be separate in larger organizations.

The process manager's accountabilities include:

- Working with the process owner to plan and coordinate all process activities
- Ensuring that all activities are carried out as required throughout the service lifecycle
- Appointing people to the required roles
- Managing resources assigned to the process
- Working with service owners and other process managers to ensure the smooth running of services
- Monitoring and reporting on process performance
- Identifying improvement opportunities
- Making improvements to the process implementation.

2.2.3.5 Process practitioner

A process practitioner is responsible for carrying out one or more process activities. In some organizations, and for some processes, the process practitioner role may be combined with the process manager role; in others there may be large numbers of practitioners carrying out different parts of the process.

The process practitioner's responsibilities typically include:

- Carrying out one or more activities of a process
- Understanding how their role contributes to the overall delivery of service and creation of value for the business
- Working with other stakeholders, such as their manager, co-workers, users and customers, to ensure that their contributions are effective
- Ensuring that inputs, outputs and interfaces for their activities are correct
- Creating or updating records to show that activities have been carried out correctly.

2.2.4 Competence and skills framework

Standardizing job titles, functions, roles and responsibilities can simplify service management and human resource management. Many service providers use a common framework of reference for competence and skills to support activities such as skill audits, planning future skill requirements, organizational development programmes and resource allocation. For example, resource and cost models are simpler and easier to use if jobs and roles are standard.

The Skills Framework for the Information Age (SFIA) is an example of a common reference model for the identification of the skills needed to develop effective IT services, information systems and technology. SFIA defines seven generic levels at which tasks can be performed, with the associated professional skills required for each level. A second dimension defines core competencies that can be combined with the professional skills. SFIA is used by many IT service providers to identify career development opportunities.

More information on SFIA can be found at www.sfia.org.uk

2.3 BEST PRACTICE

Organizations often benchmark themselves against peers and seek to close gaps in capabilities. One way to close such gaps is by adopting best practices.

Practice is a way of working, or a way in which work must be done. Practices can include activities, processes, functions, standards and guidelines.

By best practice we mean proven practices that have been successfully used by multiple organizations.

There are several sources for best practices, including:

- Standards
- Public frameworks
- Industry practices
- Academic research
- Training and education
- Internal experience.

ITIL is the most widely recognized and trusted source of best-practice guidance in the area of IT service management.

ISO/IEC 20000 provides a formal and international standard for organizations seeking to have their service management capabilities audited and certified. While ISO/IEC 20000 is a standard to be achieved and maintained, ITIL offers a body of knowledge useful for achieving the standard.

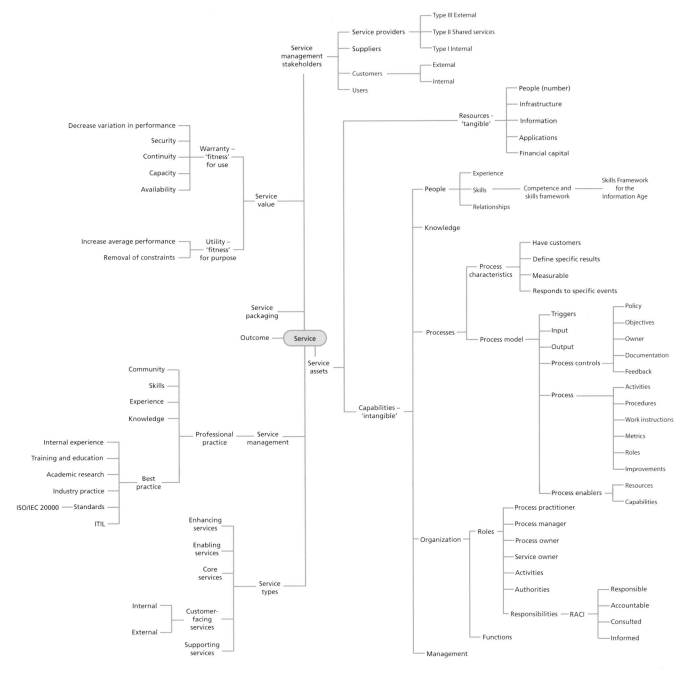

Figure 2.7 Overview of Chapter 2

2.4 SAMPLE QUESTIONS

1 Which of the following is the BEST definition of a function?

   a It is specialized to perform only one task as a separate entity

   b It is self-contained with capabilities and resources necessary for its performance

   c It is repeatable and becomes manageable

   d It is performance driven and must be able to be measured

2 A support analyst has a 'C' and 'R' against their name in the RACI matrix for the process of incident management. What does this mean?

   a They are the **customer contact** and are **responsible**

   b They will need to be **consulted** and are **responsible**

   c They will need to be **consulted** and are **retained**

   d They will need to be **communicated** to, and are **registered**

3 Which of the following activities is a process practitioner responsible for?

   1 Documenting and publicizing the process

   2 Carrying out the process activities

   3 Meeting the required key performance indicators (KPIs)

   4 Creating or updating records to show that activities have been carried out correctly

   a 1 and 3 only

   b 2 and 3 only

   c 2, 3 and 4 only

   d All of the above

4 Which of the following is a service owner accountable for?

   a Carrying out the operational activities to support the service

   b Ownership of a service regardless of its underpinning components

   c Ownership of a service for all the internally managed components of that service

   d Ensuring that the targets contained within a service level agreement are met

5 Which of the following is the BEST definition of a supporting service?

   a A service that is delivered between departments or business units in the same organization

   b A service that is delivered to external customers

   c A service that is not directly used by the business, but is required to provide the overall service

   d A service that is provided by an internal service provider

ITIL and the service lifecycle

3   ITIL and the service lifecycle

ITIL is a set of best-practice publications for IT service management. Owned by the Cabinet Office (part of HM Government in the United Kingdom), ITIL gives guidance to all types of service providers on the provision of quality IT services and the processes, functions and other capabilities needed to support them.

3.1   THE ITIL SERVICE MANAGEMENT PRACTICES

ITIL is the most widely recognized framework for IT service management in the world. In the 25 years since it was commenced, ITIL has evolved and changed its breadth and depth from a specialized set of service management topics with a focus on functions, to a process-based framework, and now to a broader set of capability-based practices providing a holistic service lifecycle.

ITIL is not a standard that has to be followed. It is guidance that should be read and understood, and used to create value for the service provider and its customers. In other words it should be *adopted* and *adapted* to work in the specific environments of the service provider in ways that meet the needs of the service provider.

The ITIL framework is based on a service lifecycle and consists of five lifecycle stages, with a core publication providing best-practice guidance for each stage. This guidance includes key principles, required processes and activities, organization and roles, technology, associated challenges, critical success factors and risks.

In addition to the core publications, there is also a complementary set of ITIL publications providing guidance specific to industry sectors, organizations types, operating models and technology architectures.

3.2   WHY ITIL?

ITIL embraces a practical approach to service management – do what works. It describes practices that enable organizations to deliver benefits, return on investment and sustained success. That is the main reason for the global success of ITIL; other reasons are that ITIL is:

■ **Vendor-neutral** ITIL service management practices are applicable in any IT organization because they are not based on any particular technology platform or industry type.
■ **Non-prescriptive** ITIL offers practices that are applicable to all types and sizes of service provider. Organizations can adopt ITIL and adapt it to meet the needs of the IT organization and their customers.
■ **Best practice** ITIL represents the learning experiences and thought leadership of the world's best-in-class service providers.

3.3   THE SERVICE LIFECYCLE

The ITIL framework is based on the five stages of the service lifecycle as shown in Figure 3.1:

■ Service strategy
■ Service design

- Service transition
- Service operation
- Continual service improvement.

Each stage addresses capabilities having direct impact on a service provider's performance.

The service lifecycle uses a hub-and-spoke design, with service strategy at the hub, and service design, transition and operation as the revolving lifecycle stages or 'spokes'. Continual service improvement surrounds and supports all stages of the service lifecycle. Each stage of the lifecycle exerts influence on the others and relies on them for inputs and feedback. In this way, a constant set of checks and balances throughout the service lifecycle ensures that as business demand changes with business need, the services can adapt and respond effectively.

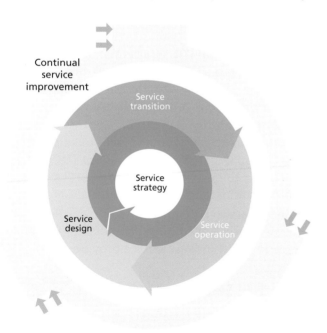

Figure 3.1 The ITIL service lifecycle

3.3.1 Service strategy

ITIL Service Strategy provides guidance on how to view service management not only as an organizational capability but as a strategic asset. It describes the principles underpinning the practice of service management which are useful for developing service management policies, guidelines and processes across the ITIL service lifecycle.

Topics covered in *ITIL Service Strategy* include the development of market spaces, characteristics of internal and external provider types, service assets, the service portfolio and implementation of strategy through the service lifecycle. Business relationship management, demand management, financial management, organizational development and strategic risks are among the other major topics.

3.3.2 Service design

ITIL Service Design provides guidance for the design and development of services and service management capabilities and practices. It covers design principles and methods for converting strategic objectives into portfolios of services and service assets. The scope of *ITIL Service Design* includes the changes and improvements necessary to increase or maintain value to customers, the continuity of services, achievement of service levels, and conformance to standards and regulations.

Topics covered in *ITIL Service Design* include design coordination, service catalogue management, service level management, availability management, capacity management, IT service continuity management, information security management and supplier management.

3.3.3 Service transition

ITIL Service Transition provides guidance for the development and improvement of capabilities for introducing new and changed services into supported environments. It describes how to transition an organization from one state to another while controlling risk and supporting organizational knowledge for decision support. It ensures that the value(s) identified in the service strategy, and encoded in service design, are effectively transitioned so that they can be realized in service operation.

Topics covered in *ITIL Service Transition* include transition planning and support, change management, service asset and configuration management, release and deployment management, service validation and testing, change evaluation and knowledge management.

3.3.4 Service operation

ITIL Service Operation provides guidance on how to maintain stability in service operation, allowing for changes in design, scale, scope and service levels. Organizations are provided with detailed process guidelines, methods and tools for use in two major control perspectives: reactive and proactive. Managers and practitioners are provided with knowledge allowing them to make better decisions in areas such as managing the availability of services, controlling demand, optimizing capacity utilization, scheduling operations, and avoiding or resolving service incidents and managing problems.

Topics covered in *ITIL Service Operation* include event management, incident management, request fulfilment, problem management and access management processes, as well as the service desk, technical management, IT operations management and application management functions.

3.3.5 Continual service improvement

ITIL Continual Service Improvement provides guidance on achieving incremental and large-scale improvements in service quality, operational efficiency and business continuity, and best practices for ensuring that the service portfolio continues to be aligned to business needs. It combines principles, practices and methods from quality management, change management and capability improvement.

Guidance is provided for linking improvement efforts and outcomes with service strategy, design, transition and operation. A closed-loop feedback system, based on the Plan-Do-Check-Act (PDCA) cycle, is established. Feedback from any stage of the service lifecycle can be used to identify improvement opportunities for any other stage of the lifecycle.

Topics covered in *ITIL Continual Service Improvement* include a seven-step improvement process, service measurement, use of metrics, baselining and maturity assessments.

Case study: service management in practice (Brigitte's experience)

Last time Brigitte stayed at the hotel, she had a conversation with the hotel manager. He happily told her the history of the hotel. It all began 10 years ago, when a number of industries moved to the area. A local family saw the opportunities for a 'bed-and-breakfast' service, but very soon the need for a hotel arose.

The family took their time in developing their strategy, including identifying the market requirements, defining what services they would deliver, creating a business case, funding, analysing the risks, getting building approval and so on.

When the strategy was clearly defined and the services described, the actual design of the hotel and its services began. This phase involved architects, designers, planners and so on.

After a year the family was ready for transition from the bed-and-breakfast facilities to the new hotel. The hotel was built and inspectors tested that the hotel fulfilled the acceptance criteria and legal regulations, personnel were hired and trained and the hotel opened.

Since then the hotel has been kept operational – through maintenance (plumbers, electricians etc.) and operational services such as waste collection, cleaning of laundry and a number of other services.

From the very beginning the hotel has continually improved its services. Small operational changes have frequently been implemented, training programmes have been improved year after year, and new services such as wireless internet access have been introduced to fulfil the changing requirements of the guests.

Recently the hotel decided to change its service strategy to become more than just a hotel; it will house a conference centre in the future. From her conversation with the manager, Brigitte realized that it is impossible to talk about one service lifecycle. In reality there are many intertwined service lifecycles with different extents and cycle frequencies.

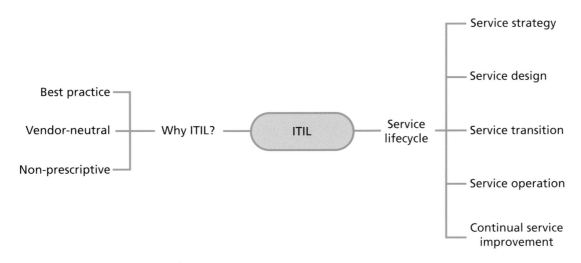

Figure 3.2 Overview of Chapter 3

Service strategy

4 Service strategy

Service strategy establishes an overall strategy for services and service management – not only as an organizational capability but as a strategic asset.

Case study: service management in practice (Brigitte's experience)

When the hotel management recently evaluated the strategy of the hotel, including the future portfolio of services, a number of alternatives were analysed:

- Building of a new wing with extra rooms
- Transformation of the hotel into a conference centre
- Expanding of the pool area to a small water world open to the public.

An analysis of the competitive position of the hotel showed that the nearest conference centre was situated about 50 kilometres away. There was a public swimming pool in the town but it had neither a slide nor a Jacuzzi.

To support the decision, management needed to identify the option that would provide the highest return on investment with the lowest risk. The first move was to prepare a business case on each of the three options.

It turned out that the most profitable investment was the conference option. The hotel management therefore crafted a plan for transforming the hotel into a conference centre to differentiate the hotel from the other alternatives in the area.

4.1 PURPOSE AND OBJECTIVES

The purpose of the service strategy stage is to define the perspective, position, plans and patterns that a service provider needs to execute in order to meet an organization's business outcomes.

The main objectives of service strategy are to provide:

- An understanding of what strategy is
- A clear identification of the definition of services and the customers who use them
- The ability to define how value is created and delivered
- A means of identifying opportunities to provide services and how to exploit them
- A clear service provision model that articulates how services will be delivered and funded, and to whom they will be delivered and for what purpose
- The means of understanding the organizational capability required to deliver the strategy
- Documentation and coordination of how service assets are used to deliver services, and how to optimize their performance
- Processes that define the strategy of the organization, which services will achieve the strategy, what level of investment will be required, at what levels of demand and the means to ensure that a working relationship exists between the customer and service provider.

4.2 SCOPE

Service strategy covers generic principles and processes of service management and how these generic principles are applied consistently to the management of IT services.

The guidance is intended for use by both internal and external service providers, and includes practices for organizations which are required to offer IT services as a profitable business, as well as those required to offer IT services to other business units within the same organization – at no profit.

Two aspects of strategy are covered in *ITIL Service Strategy*:

■ Defining a strategy whereby a service provider will deliver services to meet a customer's business outcomes
■ Defining a strategy for how to manage those services.

The following processes are within the scope of service strategy:

■ Strategy management for IT services
■ Service portfolio management
■ Financial management for IT services
■ Demand management
■ Business relationship management.

4.3 BUSINESS VALUE

Adopting and implementing consistent approaches for service strategy will:

■ Enable the service provider to link its activities to outcomes that are critical to the customers. As a result, the service provider will be seen to be contributing to the value (and not just the costs) of the organization.

■ Enable the service provider to have a clear understanding of what types and levels of service will make its customers successful, and then organize itself optimally to deliver and support those services.
■ Enable the service provider to respond quickly and effectively to changes in the business environment, ensuring increased competitive advantage over time.
■ Support the creation and maintenance of a portfolio of services that will enable the business to achieve positive return on its investment in services.
■ Facilitate functional and transparent communication between the customer and the service provider.

4.4 KEY PRINCIPLES

4.4.1 Value

The value of a service is the level to which that service meets a customer's expectations. Unlike products, services do not have much intrinsic value. The value of a service comes from what it enables someone to do. Based on this insight, some of the main characteristics of service value are:

■ Value is defined by the customer
■ Customers select the services that represent the best mix of features at the price they are willing to pay
■ Customers measure service value in terms of how the service helps them to achieve their objectives
■ Value changes over time and according to circumstances.

Therefore, understanding the value of IT requires three pieces of information:

- What services does IT provide?
- What do the services achieve?
- How much do the services cost?

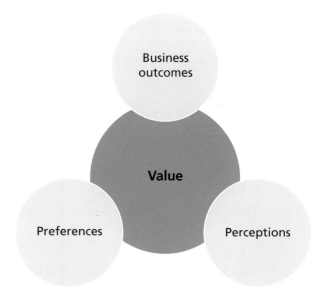

Figure 4.1 Components of value

> **Case study: service management in practice (Brigitte's experience)**
>
> Brigitte notices the information pamphlet that the hotel has left on the table in her room. It contains a number of services such as a wake-up call, parking, laundry service, dining and childcare as well as descriptive attributes of the services such as the number of television channels, cleaning of the room and breakfast times.
>
> Brigitte finds most of the services valuable, even though she doesn't need the childcare service on this occasion. But to Brigitte the described services are only a part of what she appreciates as a hotel guest. For her it is as important that the hotel is situated close to her temporary workplace, that the staff are kind and obliging, that her balcony has a beautiful view over the Alps and that the hotel respects her preference for vegetarian food.

Customers do not buy services. They buy the fulfilment of particular needs. What counts is quality as this is perceived by customers. The value of a service is therefore determined by what the customer prefers (preferences), what the customer perceives (perceptions) and what the customer actually gets (business outcomes) (see Figure 4.1).

Consequently, service providers have to demonstrate business outcomes, influence perceptions and respond to preferences.

Although a service provider is not able to decide the value of a service, it is able to influence how the value of the service is perceived by the customers. Figure 4.2 illustrates how customers perceive value.

The starting point for customer perception is the reference value. This could be based on what the customer has heard about the service, or the fact that the customer is currently doing the activity themselves, or some previous experience of that or a similar service. An example of reference value is the baseline that customers maintain on the cost of in-house services, i.e. the do-it-yourself (DIY) strategy.

The positive difference of the service is based on the perceived additional benefits and gains provided by the service provider. These differences are based on the additional warranty and utility that the service provider is able to deliver.

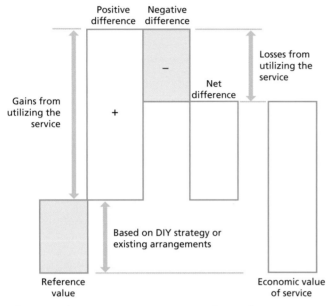

Figure 4.2 How customers perceive value

The negative difference of the service is the perception of what the customer would lose by investing in the service. For example, they might perceive some quality issues or hidden costs.

The net difference is the actual perception that the customer has of how much better (or worse) the service is than the reference value after discounting the negative difference. This is the area that will drive the customer's decision to invest in the service or not.

The economic value is the total value that the customer perceives the service to deliver. It includes the reference value plus (or minus) the net difference of the service they receive, and is measured by the customer in the ability of the service to meet their desired outcomes.

However, what the customer values is frequently different from what the IT organization believes it provides.

4.4.2 Patterns of business activity

Every time a business activity is performed, it generates demand for services. However, services cannot be produced in advance of when they are consumed. Therefore it is essential to synchronize supply and demand.

> **Case study: service management in practice (Brigitte's experience)**
>
> Brigitte takes a closer look at the flyer next to the telephone. She notices that the hotel offers a special family discount in August. She can't help but wonder why the hotel reduces its prices during the holiday season, a time when the hotel should appeal to tourists in the area.
>
> Next time she passes the reception she decides to ask the receptionist why the hotel offers a family discount in August. He answers that very few tourists have chosen to stay at the hotel in August in the last two years. The hotel management therefore discussed the situation based on that pattern and identified three possible solutions:
>
> ■ Lowering the prices for families to attract tourists
> ■ Introducing new services to attract tourists (e.g. expanding the pool area to create a small water world)
> ■ Closing the hotel for one month.

Customer assets such as people, processes and applications all perform business activities, and this activity will tend to be performed in patterns.

For example a consulting company relies on a timesheet service to bill consultants' time. Since most consultants complete their timesheets for the entire week at the end of the week, the later it is in the week, the more critical the service, and the more it is utilized. Consultants may need to be encouraged to log their time at the end of each day, or the beginning of the next day.

Since services often directly support one or more patterns of business activity (PBA) it is important that the patterns are properly understood and aligned to services.

Definition

Pattern of business activity (PBA) is a workload profile of one or more business activities. Patterns of business activity are used to help the IT service provider understand and plan for different levels of business activity.

Once a pattern of business activity has been identified, a PBA profile should be drawn up and details about the PBA documented. The following items need to be documented:

- **Classification** This indicates the type of PBA, and could refer to where it originates (user or automated), the type and impact of outcomes supported, and the type of workload supported.
- **Attributes** Such as frequency, volume, location and duration.
- **Requirements** Such as performance, security, availability, privacy, latency or tolerance for delays.
- **Service asset requirements** Design teams will draft a utilization profile for each PBA in terms of what resources it uses, and when and how much of each resource is utilized. If the quantity of resources is known and the pattern of utilization is known, the capacity management process will be able to ensure that resources are available to meet the demand – provided this stays within the forecast range.

4.4.3 Service portfolio

Case study: service management in practice (Brigitte's experience)

The delivery of the hotel services requires extensive knowledge about customers and contracts, as well as supporting services and assets such as furniture and equipment, staff members, suppliers and processes. To manage this knowledge, the hotel established a number of supporting systems some years ago, including:

- A register of services and their interdependencies
- A customer catalogue presenting the services provided by the hotel
- Service level agreements with travel agencies and larger companies
- A configuration database containing data for all relevant equipment, people, suppliers and processes that underpin the provided services.

The register of services has since supported the management in deciding which services to offer or invest in, e.g. overnight stay, dining or conference services. The register contains all the services provided to the customers and suggestions for new or changed services as well as supporting services such as laundry cleaning, internet access, pool cleaning and waste collection.

The customer catalogue is aimed at the customers and guests. When Brigitte planned her trip to Switzerland, she looked up the hotel on the internet. On the hotel's homepage she found information on the services provided:

- Overnight stay
  - Single guest room, €100 per night
  - Double guest room, €150 per night

- Suite (with table and free internet connection), €170 per night
- Executive room (with separate bedroom and living room), €200 per night
■ Dinner at the restaurant
  - Two courses (€30 per person)
  - Three courses (€40 per person)
■ Swimming pool (€5 per hour – free for guests at the hotel).

As Brigitte was pleased with the hotel services, she ordered a suite.

A service portfolio (i.e. the register in the hotel case) describes a provider's services in terms of business value. It articulates business needs and the provider's response to those needs.

Definition

The **service portfolio** is the complete set of services that are managed by a service provider.

The service portfolio represents the commitments and investments made by a service provider across all customers, market spaces and stages of the service lifecycle. The portfolio management approach helps managers to prioritize investments and improve the allocation of resources (see Figure 4.3).

The service portfolio is used to manage the entire lifecycle of all services, including:

■ Service pipeline (proposed or in development)
■ Service catalogue (live or available for deployment)
■ Retired services.

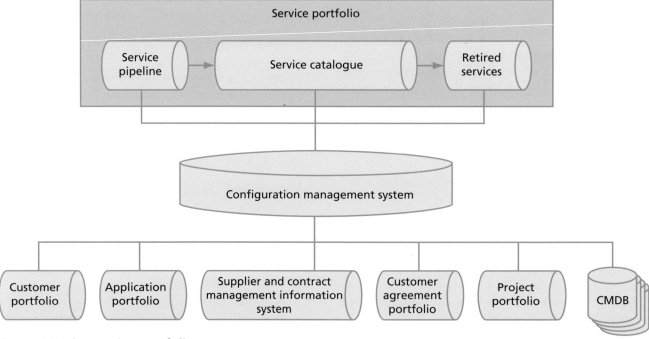

Figure 4.3 The service portfolio

The portfolio also includes third-party services, which are an integral part of service offerings to customers. Some third-party services are visible to the customers whereas others are not.

By acting as the basis of a decision framework, a service portfolio either clarifies or helps to clarify the following strategic questions:

- Why should a customer buy these services?
- Why should they buy these services from us?
- What are the pricing or chargeback models?
- What are our strengths and weaknesses, priorities and risks?
- How should our resources and capabilities be allocated?

Case study: service management in practice (Brigitte's experience)

The register of services was supposed to support the management of the hotel in answering questions such as:

- What value does an overnight stay at our hotel provide to the guests compared with similar rival hotels?
- Which supporting services, resources and capabilities are needed to provide the conference service?
- What risks are associated with dining services?

As the register became more and more complete and reliable over time, it also became more and more critical as a means to support the hotel management in making the right decisions on the optimal use of the available resources and capabilities.

Not only does the hotel maintain a register of all its services, including the services that are provided to the guests as well as underpinning services such as cleaning and cooking. It also identifies and maintains the relationships between the services. To provide an overnight stay, for example, the hotel needs to provide cleaning and (if a guest requests it) wireless internet as well.

4.4.4 Service catalogue

The service catalogue (i.e. the customer catalogue in the hotel case) is the only part of the service portfolio published to customers, and it is used to support the sale and delivery of IT services. The service catalogue includes information about deliverables, prices, contact points, ordering and request processes.

Definition

A **service catalogue** is a database or structured document with information about all live IT services, including those available for deployment.

The service catalogue is part of the service portfolio and contains information about two types of IT service: customer-facing services that are visible to the business; and supporting services required by the service provider to deliver customer-facing services.

When service providers have many customers or serve many businesses, there may be multiple service catalogue views projected from the service portfolio.

It is recommended that a service provider, at the minimum, defines two different views, each one focusing on one type of service: a view for

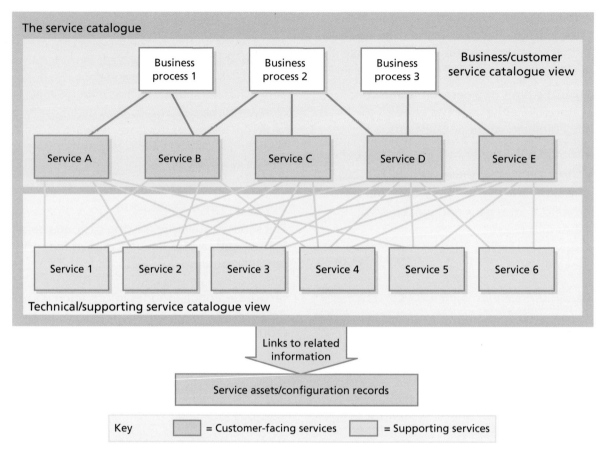

Figure 4.4 A two-view service catalogue

customers that shows the customer-facing services, and a second view for the IT service provider showing all the supporting services. Figure 4.4 shows a service catalogue with two views.

Some organizations project more than two views. There is no correct or suggested number of views an organization should project. The number of views projected will depend upon the audiences to be addressed and the uses to which the catalogue will be put. Figure 4.5 shows a service catalogue with three views:

■ **Wholesale customer view** This contains details of all the IT services delivered to wholesale customers (customer-facing services), together with relationships to the customers they support.
■ **Retail customer view** This contains details of all the IT services delivered to retail customers (customer-facing services), together with relationships to the customers they support.

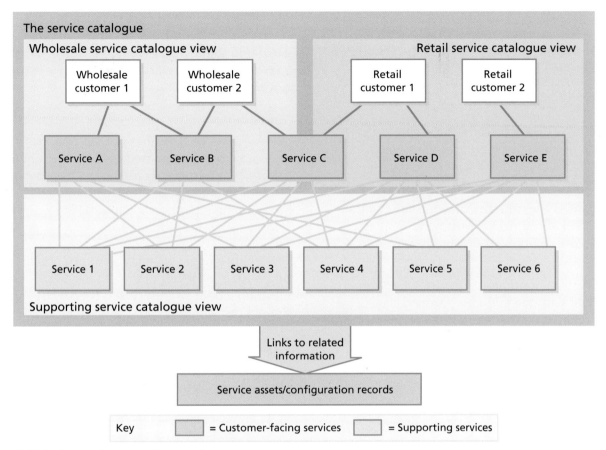

Figure 4.5 A three-view service catalogue

■ **Supporting services view** This contains details of all the supporting IT services, together with relationships to the customer-facing services they underpin and the components, configuration items (CIs) and other supporting services necessary to support the provision of the service to the customers.

4.4.5 Business case

A service provider will need to make decisions on what service management initiatives it wishes to invest in. The business case for these investments is key to this decision-making process.

A business case is a decision support and planning tool. It describes the objectives and the likely outcomes of a business decision. The outcomes can take on qualitative and quantitative dimensions.

> **Definition**
>
> A **business case** is a justification for a significant item of expenditure. It includes information about costs, benefits, options, issues, risks and possible problems.

The business case articulates the objectives of the initiative and the specific business impacts (costs, risks and benefits) that the initiative is expected to generate (see Table 4.1).

The financial consequence of a decision, typically in the form of return on investment (ROI), is often a core component of a business case.

A well-rounded business case also covers an analysis of the desired non-financial business impacts associated with the initiative, forming clear linkages between these non-financial impacts and a recognized business objective. This analysis may use the value on investment (VOI) technique.

4.4.6 Governance

Governance is the single overarching area that ties IT and the business together, and services are one way of ensuring that the organization is able to execute that governance. Governance is what defines the common directions, policies and rules that both the business and IT use to conduct business.

Many IT service management strategies fail because they try to build structures or processes according to how they would *like* the organization to work instead of working within the existing governance structures.

> **Definition**
>
> **Governance** ensures that policies and strategy are actually implemented, and that required processes are correctly followed. Governance includes defining roles and responsibilities, measuring and reporting, and taking actions to resolve any issues identified.

Governance works to apply a consistently managed approach at all levels of the organization – first by ensuring a clear strategy is set, then by defining the policies whereby the strategy will be achieved. The policies also define boundaries, or what the organization may not do as part of its operations.

According to the standard for corporate governance of IT, ISO/IEC 38500, governance needs to be able to evaluate, direct and monitor the strategy, policies and plans.

Table 4.1 Example of a business case structure

A. Introduction	Presents the business objectives addressed by the service.
B. Methods and assumptions	Defines the boundaries of the business case, such as time period, whose costs and whose benefits.
C. Business impacts	The financial and non-financial business case results.
D. Risks and contingencies	The probability that alternative results will emerge.
E. Recommendations	Specific actions recommended.

4.4.7 Management of risk

Risk assessment and risk management should be applied to identify and mitigate risks within all parts of the service lifecycle.

4.4.7.1 Risk

> **Definition**
>
> **Risk** is a possible event that could cause harm or loss, or affect the ability to achieve objectives.

A risk is measured by the probability of a threat, the vulnerability of the asset to that threat, and the impact it would have if it occurred (see Figure 4.6).

Risk can also be defined as uncertainty of outcome, and can be used in the context of measuring the probability of positive outcomes as well as negative outcomes.

4.4.7.2 Risk assessment

Risk assessment is concerned with gathering information about exposure to risk so that the organization carrying out the risk assessment can make appropriate decisions and manage risk appropriately. Risk assessment is concerned with analysing the value of assets to the business, identifying threats to those assets, and evaluating how vulnerable each asset is to those threats. Risk assessment can be quantitative (based on numerical data) or qualitative.

4.4.7.3 Risk management

Risk management involves having processes in place to monitor risks, access to reliable and up-to-date information about risks, the right balance of control in place to deal with those risks, and decision-making processes supported by a framework of risk analysis and evaluation.

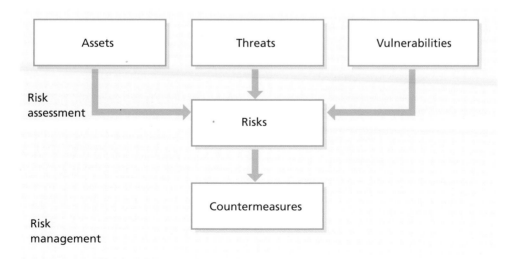

Figure 4.6 Risk assessment and management

Risk management also involves the identification, selection and adoption of countermeasures justified by the identified risks.

4.5 PROCESSES

The ITIL Foundation syllabus covers the following service strategy processes:

■ Service portfolio management
■ Financial management for IT services
■ Business relationship management.

4.5.1 Service portfolio management

Service portfolio management is the process responsible for managing the service portfolio. Service portfolio management ensures that the service provider has the right mix of services to meet required business outcomes at an appropriate level of investment. Service portfolio management considers services in terms of the business value that they provide.

4.5.1.1 Purpose and objectives

The purpose of service portfolio management is to ensure that the service provider has the right mix of services to balance the investment in IT with the ability to meet business outcomes. It tracks the investment in services throughout their lifecycle and works with other service management processes to ensure that the appropriate returns are being achieved. In addition, it ensures that services are clearly defined and linked to the achievement of business outcomes, thus ensuring that all design, transition and operation activities are aligned to the value of the services.

The objectives of service portfolio management are to:

■ Provide a process and mechanisms to enable an organization to investigate and decide on which services to provide, based on an analysis of the potential return and acceptable level of risk.
■ Maintain the definitive portfolio of services provided, articulating the business needs each service meets and the business outcomes it supports.
■ Provide a mechanism for the organization to evaluate how services enable it to achieve its strategy, and to respond to changes in its internal or external environments.
■ Control which services are offered, under what conditions and at what level of investment.
■ Track the investment in services throughout their lifecycle, thus enabling the organization to evaluate its strategy, as well as its ability to execute against that strategy.
■ Analyse which services are no longer viable and when they should be retired.

4.5.1.2 Scope

The scope of service portfolio management is all services a service provider plans to deliver, those currently delivered and those that have been withdrawn from service.

Internal service providers will need to work with the business units in the organization to link each service to the business outcomes before they can compare investment with returns. External service providers tend to assess value more directly, as each service needs to be able to generate revenue directly, or support revenue-generating services.

Service portfolio management evaluates the value of services throughout their lifecycles, and must be able to appraise what newer services have offered in comparison with the retired services they have replaced.

4.5.2 Financial management for IT services

Financial management for IT services is the process responsible for managing an IT service provider's budgeting, accounting and charging requirements.

> **Case study: service management in practice (Brigitte's experience)**
>
> Next door to the hotel a new restaurant opened a couple of months ago. As a consequence the hotel restaurant has more than halved its number of guests. The staff level in the restaurant has been adapted accordingly. At the weekly management team meeting the situation is being discussed. It is a very emotional discussion – should the restaurant be closed or not? The financial manager is asked to prepare a financial assessment of the restaurant.
>
> At the next meeting the financial manager presents his analysis: the restaurant is only just profitable. But the hotel management decides to keep it, as it provides a more seamless service provision to the guests if the hotel runs its own restaurant. Further, the hotel is expected to expand during the coming years: more rooms are planned and a conference centre will generate extra custom for the restaurant.

4.5.2.1 Purpose and objectives

The purpose of financial management for IT services is to secure the appropriate level of funding to design, develop and deliver services that meet the strategy of the organization. Financial management for IT services identifies the balance between the cost and quality of service and maintains the balance of supply and demand between the service provider and its customers.

The objectives of financial management for IT services include:

- Defining and maintaining a framework to identify, manage and communicate the cost of providing services.
- Evaluating the financial impact of new or changed strategies on the service provider.
- Securing funding to manage the provision of services.
- Facilitating good stewardship of service and customer assets to ensure that the organization meets its objectives.
- Understanding the relationship between expenses and income and ensuring that the two are balanced according to the organization's financial policies.
- Managing and reporting expenditure on service provision on behalf of the organization's stakeholders.
- Executing the financial policies and practices in the provision of services.
- Accounting for money spent on the creation, delivery and support of services.
- Forecasting the financial requirements for the organization to be able to meet its service commitments to its customers, and compliance with regulatory and legislative requirements.
- Where appropriate, defining a framework to recover the costs of service provision from the customer.

4.5.2.2 Scope

Financial management is normally a well-established and well-understood part of any organization. Professional accountants set financial policies, budgeting procedures, financial reporting standards, accounting practices and revenue generation or cost recovery rules. However, financial management for IT services is a specialized area that requires an understanding of the world of finance and business as well as the world of technology.

Financial management for IT services consists of three main processes:

- **Budgeting** This is the process of predicting and controlling the income and expenditure of money within the organization. Budgeting consists of a periodic negotiation cycle to set budgets (usually annual) and monthly monitoring of the current budgets.
- **Accounting** This is the process that enables the IT organization to account fully for the way its money is spent (particularly the ability to identify costs by customer, by service and by activity). It usually involves accounting systems including ledgers, charts of accounts, journals etc. and should be overseen by someone trained in accountancy.
- **Charging** This is the process required to bill customers for the services supplied to them. This requires sound IT accounting practices and systems.

4.5.3 Business relationship management

Business relationship management is the process responsible for maintaining a positive relationship with customers. Business relationship management identifies customer needs and ensures that the service provider is able to meet these needs with an appropriate catalogue of services.

4.5.3.1 Purpose and objectives

The purpose of the business relationship management process is two-fold:

- To establish and maintain a business relationship between the service provider and the customer based on understanding the customer and their business needs.
- To identify customer needs and ensure that the service provider is able to meet these needs as business needs change over time and between circumstances. Business relationship management ensures that customer expectations do not exceed what they are willing to pay for, and that the service provider is able to meet the customer's expectations before agreeing to deliver the service.

The objectives of business relationship management include:

- Ensure that the service provider understands the customer's perspective of service, and is therefore able to prioritize its services and service assets appropriately.
- Ensure high levels of customer satisfaction, indicating that the service provider is meeting the customer's requirements.
- Establish and maintain a constructive relationship between the service provider and the customer, based on understanding the customer and their business drivers.
- Identify changes to the customer environment that could potentially impact the type, level or utilization of services provided.
- Identify technology trends that could potentially impact the type, level or utilization of services provided.
- Establish and articulate business requirements for new services or changes to existing services.

- Work with customers to ensure that services and service levels are able to deliver value.
- Mediate in cases where there are conflicting requirements for services from different business units.
- Establish formal complaint and escalation processes for the customer.

4.5.3.2 Scope

For internal service providers, business relationship management is typically executed between a senior representative from IT (larger organizations may have dedicated business relationship managers) and senior managers (customers) from the business units. Here the emphasis is on aligning the objectives of the business with the activity of the service provider.

In external service providers, business relationship management is often executed by a separate and dedicated function of business relationship managers or account managers – each one dedicated to a customer or group of smaller customers. The emphasis here is on maximizing contract value through customer satisfaction.

The relationships between business relationship management and other service management processes must be clearly defined. The main criterion for setting these boundaries is that business relationship management focuses on the actual relationship between the service provider and its customers and the levels of customer satisfaction, whereas the other processes focus on the services themselves and the extent to which they meet the stated requirements.

Table 4.2 Differences between business relationship management and service level management

	Business relationship management	Service level management
Purpose	To establish and maintain a business relationship between the service provider and the customer based on understanding the customer and their business needs. To identify customer needs (utility and warranty) and ensure that the service provider is able to meet these needs.	To negotiate service level agreements (warranty terms) with customers and ensure that all service management processes, operational level agreements and underpinning contracts are appropriate for the agreed service level targets.
Focus	Strategic and tactical – the focus is on the overall relationship between the service provider and its customer, and which services the service provider will deliver to meet customer needs.	Tactical and operational – the focus is on reaching agreement on the level of service that will be delivered for new and existing services, and whether the service provider will be able to meet those agreements.
Primary measure	Customer satisfaction, also an improvement in the customer's intention to better use and pay for the service. Another metric is whether customers are willing to recommend the service to other (potential) customers.	Achieving agreed levels of service (which leads to customer satisfaction).

A good example of the differences between business relationship management and other service management processes is that of service level management. These distinctions are summarized in Table 4.2.

4.6 SAMPLE QUESTIONS

1 Which of the following activities is NOT a key part of the service strategy lifecycle stage?

a Establishing the service design package (SDP)

b Setting policies and objectives

c Agreements on resource allocation

d Establishing the service portfolio

2 Which of the following are valid components of value?

1 Whether the service achieves its agreed outcomes

2 Customer perceptions of the delivered service

3 Customer preferences of the service

4 Understanding the risk of the service

a 1 only

b 1 and 4 only

c 1, 2 and 3 only

d All of the above

3 When a service is in its requirements stage, where should it be placed in the service portfolio?

a In the service catalogue

b As a retired service

c In the pipeline

d It should not go in the service portfolio at this stage

4 Which of the following should be included in the business case?

1 Business impact

2 Risks and contingencies

3 Costs and benefits

4 Solution specification

a 1, 2 and 4 only

b 3 and 4 only

c 1, 2 and 3 only

d All of the above

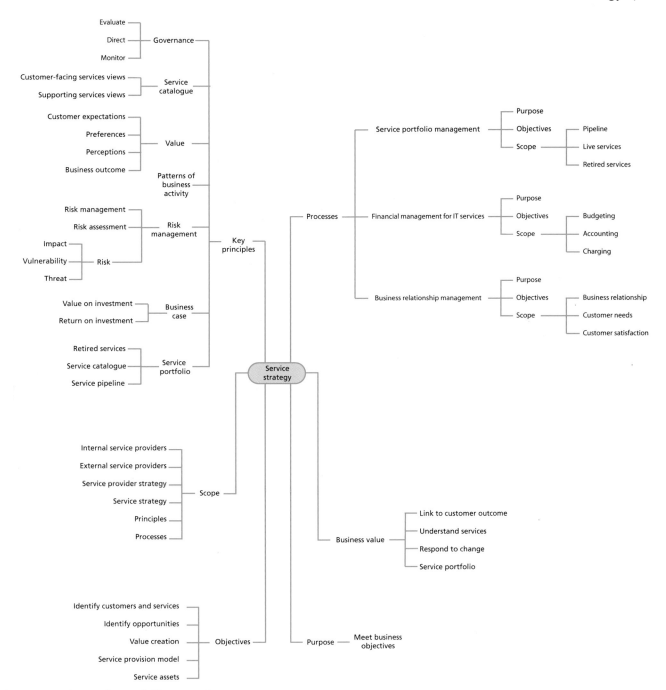

Figure 4.7 Overview of Chapter 4

Service design

5 Service design

The service design stage takes business requirements and creates services, their supporting practices and management tools which meet business demands for quality, reliability and flexibility.

Case study: service management in practice (Brigitte's experience)

Later that afternoon Brigitte notices a group of local people in the hotel lobby. She can't help being curious and asks the first one she meets what is going on. It turns out that the hotel has arranged a meeting for businesses in the area to discuss their requirements for local conference services and facilities.

The hotel manager later explains that a local architect has been selected to design the facilities based on input from the meeting as well as requirements collected through a guest survey carried out in past months.

But he also stresses that the conference building and facilities are probably the smallest challenges when designing the new conference service. A project manager has therefore temporarily been hired to redesign processes, employ people, assign responsibilities, develop sales material and so on.

5.1 PURPOSE AND OBJECTIVES

The purpose of the service design stage of the lifecycle is to:

- Design IT services, together with the governing IT practices, processes and policies, to realize the service provider's strategy
- Facilitate the introduction of these services into supported environments ensuring quality service delivery, customer satisfaction and cost-effective service provision.

The main objective of service design is to design IT services so effectively that minimal improvement during their lifecycle will be required.

5.2 SCOPE

Service design covers:

- Alignment of IT services and solutions with business requirements
- Principles of service design
- The concept of a service design package
- Methods, practices and tools to achieve excellence in service design.

The following processes are within the scope of service design:

- Design coordination
- Service catalogue management
- Service level management
- Availability management
- Capacity management
- IT service continuity management
- Information security management
- Supplier management.

5.3 BUSINESS VALUE

With good service design it will be possible to deliver quality and cost-effective services, and ensure that the business requirements are being met consistently.

Adopting and implementing consistent approaches for service design will:

- **Reduce total cost of ownership** Cost of ownership can be minimized if all aspects of services, processes and technology are designed properly and implemented against the design.
- **Improve quality and consistency of service** Both service and operational quality will be enhanced and services will be designed within the corporate strategy, architectures and constraints.
- **Ease the implementation of new or changed services** Integrated and full service designs and the production of comprehensive service design packages will support effective and efficient transitions.
- **Improve effectiveness of service management and IT processes** Processes will be designed with optimal quality and cost effectiveness.
- **Improve service alignment** Involvement from the conception of the service ensures that new or changed services match business needs, with services designed to meet service level requirements.

5.4 KEY PRINCIPLES

5.4.1 People, processes, products and partners – the four Ps

Many designs, plans and projects fail through a lack of preparation and management. Good service design is dependent on preparing and planning the effective and efficient use of the 'four Ps': people, processes, products and partners (see Figure 5.1).

When designing a new or changed service, service design focuses on ensuring that the four Ps are taken into account at every stage throughout the service lifecycle. This is achieved through the five major design aspects described in the next section.

> **Case study: service management in practice (Brigitte's experience)**
>
> Looking out of the window, Brigitte notices a service technician entering the hotel from the back entrance. On the car it says 'Electrician – call Jacob at (4) 270435'. Brigitte wonders whether Jacob is a regular supplier to the hotel or just an electrician called in to solve a specific issue.
>
> She realizes that management has to decide whether they want to hire people (employees) to get a job done or to contract with partners like Jacob.
>
> Irrespective of whether they hire their own people or use external partners, management has to decide how the business should be run and describe the related processes.

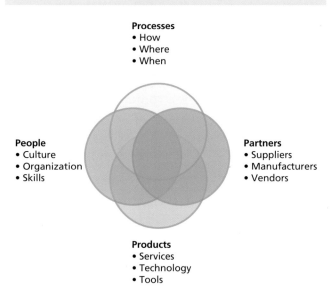

Processes
- How
- Where
- When

People
- Culture
- Organization
- Skills

Partners
- Suppliers
- Manufacturers
- Vendors

Products
- Services
- Technology
- Tools

Figure 5.1 The four Ps

5.4.2 The five aspects of service design

An overall, integrated approach should be adopted for the design activities, covering a holistic, result-driven design of:

- The service solutions for new or changed services, including all of the functional requirements, resources and capabilities needed and agreed
- Management information systems and tools, especially the service portfolio for the management of services through their lifecycle
- Technology architectures and management architectures
- The processes required to identify, design, transition, operate, support, maintain and improve new or changed services
- The measurement methods and metrics for the services, architectures and their constituent components, and the processes.

5.4.3 Service design package

A service design package (SDP) should be produced during the design stage for each new service, major change to a service or removal of a service, or changes to the 'service design package' itself.

> **Definition**
>
> A **service design package** is a document or documents defining all aspects of an IT service and its requirements through each stage of its lifecycle.

A service design package is produced for each new IT service, major change or IT service retirement. It must contain everything necessary for the subsequent testing, introduction and operation of the solution or service. The contents may include elements such as:

- Business requirements
- Service functional requirements
- Service level requirements
- Service and operational management requirements
- Service design and topology
- Organizational readiness assessment
- Service transition plan
- Service operational acceptance plan
- Service acceptance criteria.

The service design package is then passed from service design to service transition and details all aspects of the service and its requirements through all of the subsequent stages of its lifecycle.

5.5 PROCESSES

The ITIL Foundation syllabus covers the following service design processes:

- Design coordination
- Service catalogue management
- Service level management
- Supplier management
- Availability management
- Capacity management
- IT service continuity management
- Information security management.

5.5.1 Design coordination

Design coordination is the process responsible for coordinating all service design activities, processes and resources. Design coordination ensures the consistent and effective design of new or changed IT services, service management information systems, architectures, technology, processes, information and metrics.

5.5.1.1 *Purpose and objectives*

The purpose of the design coordination process is to ensure the goals and objectives of the service design stage are met by providing and maintaining a single point of coordination and control for all activities and processes within this stage of the service lifecycle.

The objectives of the design coordination process are to:

- Ensure the consistent design of appropriate services, service management information systems, architectures, technology, processes, information and metrics to meet current and evolving business outcomes and requirements
- Coordinate all design activities across projects, changes, suppliers and support teams, and manage schedules, resources and conflicts where required
- Plan and coordinate the resources and capabilities required to design new or changed services
- Produce service design packages (SDPs) based on service charters and change requests
- Ensure that appropriate service designs and/or SDPs are produced and that they are handed over to service transition as agreed
- Manage the quality criteria, requirements and handover points between the service design stage and service strategy and service transition
- Ensure that all service models and service solution designs conform to strategic, architectural, governance and other corporate requirements
- Improve the effectiveness and efficiency of service design activities and processes
- Ensure that all parties adopt a common framework of standard, reusable design practices in the form of activities, processes and supporting systems, whenever appropriate

- Monitor and improve the performance of the service design lifecycle stage.

5.5.1.2 *Scope*

The scope of the design coordination process includes all design activity, particularly all new or changed service solutions that are being designed for transition into (or out of, in the case of a service retirement) the live environment. Some design efforts will be part of a project, whereas others will be managed through the change process alone without a formally defined project.

The design coordination process includes:

- Assisting and supporting each project or other change through all the service design activities and processes
- Maintaining policies, guidelines, standards, budgets, models, resources and capabilities for service design activities and processes
- Coordinating, prioritizing and scheduling all service design resources to satisfy conflicting demands from all projects and changes
- Planning and forecasting the resources needed for the future demand for service design activities
- Reviewing, measuring and improving the performance of all service design activities and processes
- Ensuring that all requirements are appropriately addressed in service designs, particularly utility and warranty requirements
- Ensuring the production of service designs and/ or service design packages and their handover to service transition.

5.5.2 Service catalogue management

Service catalogue management is the process responsible for providing and maintaining the service catalogue and for ensuring that it is available to those who are authorized to access it.

5.5.2.1 Purpose and objectives

The purpose of the service catalogue management process is to provide and maintain a single source of consistent information on all operational services and those being prepared to be run operationally, and to ensure that it is widely available to those who are authorized to access it.

The objectives of the service catalogue management process are to:

- Manage the information contained within the service catalogue
- Ensure that the service catalogue is accurate and reflects the current details, status, interfaces and dependencies of all services that are being run, or being prepared to run, in the live environment, according to the defined policies
- Ensure that the service catalogue is made available to those approved to access it in a manner that supports their effective and efficient use of service catalogue information
- Ensure that the service catalogue supports the evolving needs of all other service management processes for service catalogue information.

5.5.2.2 Scope

The scope of the service catalogue management process is to provide and maintain accurate information on all services that are being transitioned or have been transitioned to the live environment. The services presented in the service catalogue may be listed individually or, more typically, some or all of the services may be presented in the form of service packages.

The service catalogue management process covers:

- Contribution to the definition of services and service packages
- Development and maintenance of service and service package descriptions appropriate for the service catalogue
- Production and maintenance of an accurate service catalogue
- Interfaces, dependencies and consistency between the service catalogue and the overall service portfolio
- Interfaces and dependencies between all services and supporting services within the service catalogue and the configuration management system (CMS)
- Interfaces and dependencies between all services, and supporting components and configuration items (CIs) within the service catalogue and the configuration management system.

5.5.3 Service level management

Service level management (SLM) is the process responsible for negotiating service level agreements and ensuring that these are met. It is responsible for ensuring that all IT service management processes, operational level agreements and underpinning contracts are appropriate for the agreed service level targets. Service level management monitors and reports on service levels, holds regular service reviews with customers, and identifies required improvements.

Case study: service management in practice (Brigitte's experience)

Last time Brigitte checked out of the hotel the receptionist had asked: 'Did your stay meet your expectations?'

Brigitte realized that she had not been aware of what she actually expected from the stay. She had ordered a suite for one night. Of course she had expected the room to be clean, to smell good, and the bed to be neither too soft nor too hard. She had furthermore expected hot milk for her morning coffee and fresh fruit as well as cheese and bread for breakfast. From the hotel homepage she had received the impression that the staff had a warm and friendly attitude towards guests. Fortunately, most of her expectations were met – except for the hot milk.

'Yes, my stay did live up to my expectations.' Brigitte noticed that the receptionist typed her answer into the computer.

Brigitte may have looked puzzled, because the receptionist had continued: 'We normally don't sign agreements with our guests documenting mutual expectations. But we often do it with the travel agencies. I am currently negotiating an agreement with a travel agency, where we discuss service levels such as restaurant opening hours and room service.'

5.5.3.1   Purpose and objectives

The purpose of the service level management (SLM) process is to ensure that all current and planned IT services are delivered to agreed achievable targets. This is accomplished through a constant cycle of negotiating, agreeing, monitoring, reporting on and reviewing IT service targets and achievements, and through instigation of actions to correct or improve the level of service delivered.

The objectives of service level management are to:

- Define, document, agree, monitor, measure, report and review the level of IT services provided and instigate corrective measures whenever appropriate
- Provide and improve the relationship and communication with the business and customers in conjunction with business relationship management
- Ensure that specific and measurable targets are developed for all IT services
- Monitor and improve customer satisfaction with the quality of service delivered
- Ensure that IT and the customers have clear and unambiguous expectations of the level of service to be delivered
- Ensure that even when all agreed targets are met, the levels of service delivered are subject to proactive, cost-effective continual improvement.

5.5.3.2   Scope

Service level management should provide a point of regular contact and communication to the customers and business managers of an organization in relation to service levels. This activity should encompass both the use of existing services and the potential future requirements for new or changed services.

Service level management needs to manage the expectations and perceptions of the business, customers and users and ensure that the quality (warranty) of service delivered by the service provider is matched to those expectations and needs. In order to do this effectively, service level management should establish and maintain service level agreements (SLAs) for all current live services and manage the level of service provided to meet the targets and quality measurements contained within the SLAs. Service level management should also produce and agree service level requirements (SLRs) for all planned new or changed services that document warranty requirements.

5.5.3.3 Basic concepts

Service level agreement

Service level agreements provide the basis for managing the relationship between the service provider and the customer.

> **Definition**
>
> A **service level agreement** (SLA) is an agreement between an IT service provider and a customer. An SLA describes the IT service, documents service level targets and specifies the responsibilities of the IT service provider and the customer. A single agreement may cover multiple IT services or multiple customers.

Service level requirement

Service level agreements are based on requirements from the customers. It is advisable to involve customers from the outset; but rather than approaching customers with a 'blank page', it may be better to produce an outline draft with potential performance targets and the management and operational requirements as a starting point for more detailed and in-depth discussion.

> **Definition**
>
> A **service level requirement** (SLR) is a customer requirement for an aspect of a service. Service level requirements are based on business objectives and are used to negotiate agreed service level targets.

The service level requirements should be an integral part of the overall service design criteria, which also include functional specifications. Service level requirements should, from the very start, form part of the testing criteria as the service progresses through the stages of design and development or procurement.

This service level requirement will gradually be refined as the service moves through its lifecycle, until it eventually becomes a pilot SLA during the early-life support period.

SLA framework

Using the service catalogue as an aid, service level management must design the most appropriate SLA structure to ensure that all services and all customers are covered in a manner best suited to the organization's needs. There are a number of potential options, including the following.

Service-based SLA

This is where an SLA covers one service, for all the customers of that service – for example, an SLA may be established for an organization's email service, covering all the customers of that service.

Customer-based SLA

This is an agreement with an individual customer group, covering all the services they use. For example, agreements may be reached with an organization's finance department covering, say, the finance system, the accounting system, the payroll system, the billing system, the procurement system and any other IT systems that they use. Customers often prefer such an agreement, as all of their requirements are covered in a single document. Only one signatory is normally required, which simplifies this issue.

MULTI-LEVEL **SLAs**

Some organizations have chosen to adopt a multi-level SLA structure as shown in Figure 5.2. For example, a three-layer structure might be arranged as follows:

- **Corporate level** Covering all the generic service level management issues appropriate to every customer throughout the organization. These issues are likely to be less volatile, so updates are less frequently required.
- **Customer level** Covering all service level management issues relevant to the particular customer group or business unit, regardless of the service being used.

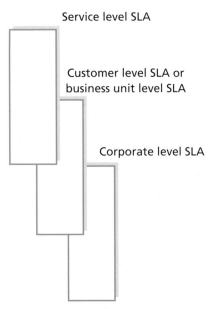

Service level SLA

Customer level SLA or business unit level SLA

Corporate level SLA

Figure 5.2 Multi-level SLAs

- **Service level** Covering all service level management issues relevant to the specific service, in relation to a specific customer group (one for each service covered by the SLA).

Operational level agreements and underpinning contracts

The service level agreements are underpinned by operational level agreements (OLAs) and underpinning contracts.

Definitions

An **operational level agreement** (OLA) is an agreement between an IT service provider and another part of the same organization. It supports the IT service provider's delivery of IT services to customers and defines the goods or services to be provided and the responsibilities of both parties.

For example, there could be an operational level agreement between:

- The IT service provider and a procurement department to obtain hardware at agreed times
- The service desk and a support group to provide incident resolution within agreed times.

An **underpinning contract** (UC) is a contract (i.e. legally binding agreement) between an IT service provider and a third party, called the supplier. The third party provides goods or services that support delivery of an IT service to a customer. The underpinning contract defines targets and responsibilities that are required to meet agreed service level targets in one or more service level agreements.

The contents of a basic underpinning contract are:

- Basic terms and conditions
- Service description and scope
- Service standards, i.e. service measures and minimum levels that constitute acceptable performance and quality
- Workload ranges
- Management information
- Responsibilities and dependencies.

Service reports

Periodic service level reports must be produced and circulated to customers and appropriate IT managers. The periodic reports should incorporate details of performance against all SLA targets, together with details of any trends or specific actions being undertaken to improve service quality.

A useful technique is to include an SLA monitoring (SLAM) chart at the beginning of a service report to give an 'at-a-glance' overview of how achievements have measured up against targets (see Figure 5.3).

Definition

A **service level agreement monitoring** (SLAM) chart is used to help monitor and report achievements against service level targets. SLAM charts are typically colour coded (red, amber and green, and sometimes referred to as RAG charts as a result) to show whether each agreed service level target has been met, missed or nearly missed during each of the previous 12 months.

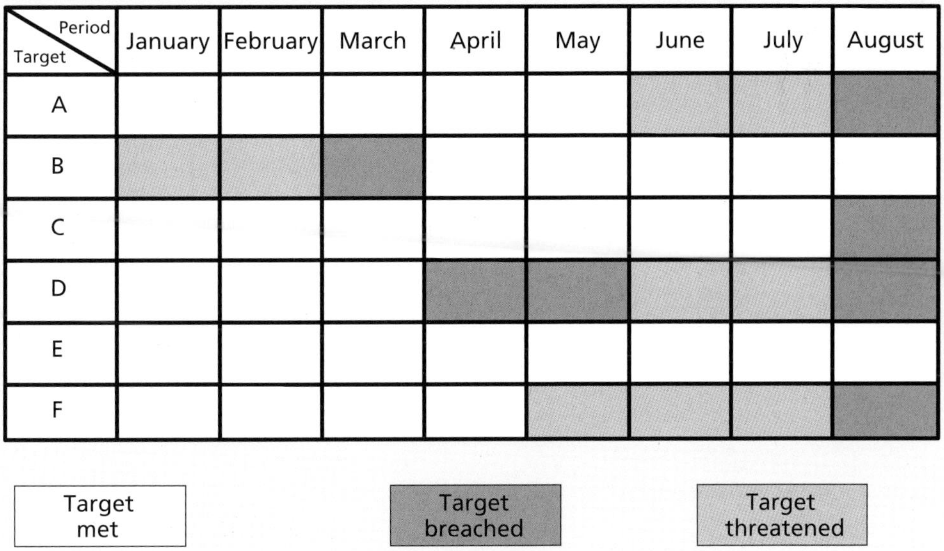

Period / Target	January	February	March	April	May	June	July	August
A						▨	▨	▨
B	▨	▨	▨					
C								▨
D				▨	▨	▨	▨	▨
E								
F					▨	▨	▨	▨

Target met	Target breached	Target threatened

Figure 5.3 Service level agreement monitoring (SLAM) chart

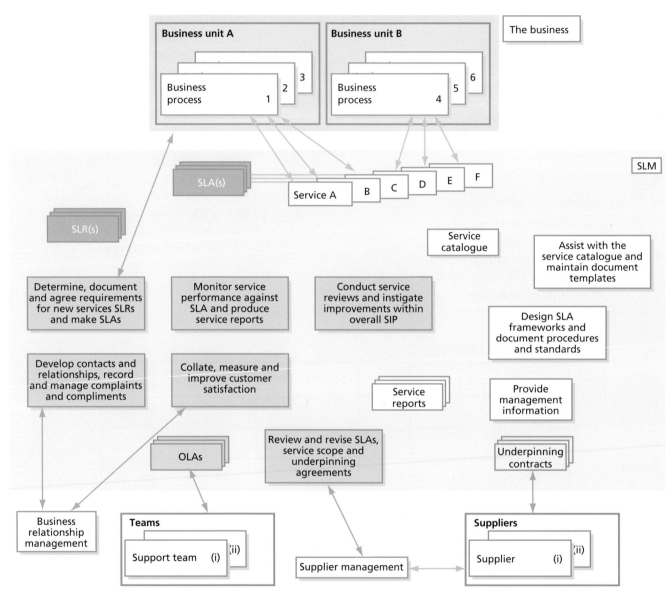

Figure 5.4 The service level management process

Service improvement plan and service review

Review meetings must be held on a regular basis with customers (or their representatives) to review the service achievement in the last period and to preview any issues for the coming period. It is normal to hold such meetings monthly or, as a minimum, quarterly.

Actions must be placed on the customer and provider as appropriate to improve weak areas where targets are not being met. All actions must be minuted, and progress should be reviewed at the next meeting to ensure that action items are being followed up and properly implemented.

This is valuable input to the service improvement plan (SIP) for the management, planning and implementation of all service and process improvements.

> **Definition**
>
> A **service improvement plan** (SIP) is a formal plan to implement improvements to a process or service.

All agreements and underpinning agreements, including SLAs, underpinning contracts and operational level agreements (OLAs), must be kept up to date. They should be reviewed periodically, at least annually, to ensure that they are still current and comprehensive, and are still aligned to business needs and strategy.

These reviews should ensure that the services covered and the targets for each are still relevant – and that nothing significant has changed that invalidates the agreement in any way.

5.5.3.4 Process activities

Service level management includes the process of planning, coordinating, drafting, agreeing, monitoring and reporting of SLAs and the ongoing review of service achievements to ensure that the required and cost-justifiable service quality is maintained and gradually improved.

The key activities within the service level management process (see Figure 5.4) include:

- Determine, negotiate, document and agree requirements for new or changed services in service level requirements, and manage and review them through the service lifecycle into SLAs for operational services
- Monitor and measure service performance achievements against targets within SLAs
- Produce service reports
- Conduct service reviews, identifying improvement opportunities for inclusion in the continual service improvement (CSI) register, and managing appropriate service improvement plans (SIPs)
- Collate, measure and improve customer satisfaction, in cooperation with business relationship management
- Review and revise SLAs, service scope and OLAs
- Assist supplier management to review and revise underpinning contracts or agreements
- Develop and document contacts and relationships with the business, customers and other stakeholders in cooperation with business relationship management
- Log and manage complaints and compliments, in cooperation with business relationship management

- Provide appropriate management information to aid performance management and demonstrate service achievement.

These other activities within the service level management process support the execution of the key activities:

- Design SLA frameworks
- Develop, maintain and operate service level management procedures
- Make available and maintain up-to-date service level management document templates and standards
- Assist with design and maintenance of the service catalogue views.

5.5.3.5 Interfaces

The most critical interfaces for the service level management process include:

- **Financial management for IT services** Supports service level management in validating the predicted cost of delivering the required service levels and managing the cost effectiveness of the service.
- **Business relationship management** Ensures that needs and priorities of the business are fully understood and that customers are involved or represented in the work of service level management.
- **Design coordination** Ensures that overall service design activities are completed successfully.
- **Service catalogue management** Provides information about services and their interfaces and dependencies to determine the SLA framework.
- **Supplier management** Works collaboratively with service level management to define, negotiate, document and agree terms of service with suppliers to support agreed service levels.
- **Availability, capacity, IT service continuity and information security management** Helps to define realistic service level targets and to ensure that achievements match targets.
- **Incident management** The ability to resolve incidents in a specified time is a key part of delivering and reporting on an agreed level of service.
- **Problem management** The occurrence of problems affects the level of service delivery measured by service level management.

Special attention should be paid to the relationship between service level management and business relationship management. While the service level management process exists to ensure that agreed achievable levels of service are provided to the customer and users, the business relationship management process is focused on a more strategic perspective. Business relationship management takes as its mission the identification of customer needs and ensuring that the service provider is able to meet the customers' needs. It focuses on the overall relationship between the service provider and the customer, working to determine which services the service provider will deliver.

5.5.4 Supplier management

Supplier management is the process responsible for obtaining value for money from suppliers, ensuring that all contracts and agreements with suppliers support the needs of the business, and that all suppliers meet their contractual commitments.

Case study: service management in practice (Brigitte's experience)

Brigitte steps out into the corridor from her room and bumps into the electrician, Jacob, who is preparing to install electronic card key locks on all the guest room doors. The hotel manager comes by to give some last-minute instructions and when he starts to leave again Brigitte asks him: 'Why don't you install the card system yourself?' The manager answers: 'This hotel is much too small to employ an electrician of its own. In this town there are only four independent electricians. Of these, one has a very bad reputation; we have also tried the other three and had the best results from Jacob. What we like best about Jacob is that he always keeps us informed about the progress of his work as well as any risks for delays. He takes responsibility for the job and strives to obtain the best result for the hotel.'

As a result of the evaluation of his work, the hotel has established a three-year contract with Jacob. The contract allows the hotel to call Jacob at all hours whenever a problem has to be resolved. On the other hand, Jacob knows that he is the hotel's first choice whenever an electrician is needed.

5.5.4.1   Purpose and objectives

The purpose of the supplier management process is to obtain value for money from suppliers and to provide seamless quality of IT service to the business by ensuring that all contracts and agreements with suppliers support the needs of the business and that all suppliers meet their contractual commitments.

The main objectives of the supplier management process are to:

- Obtain value for money from suppliers and contracts
- Ensure that contracts with suppliers are aligned to business needs, and support and align with agreed targets in SLAs, in conjunction with service level management
- Manage relationships with suppliers
- Manage supplier performance
- Negotiate and agree contracts with suppliers and manage them through their lifecycle
- Maintain a supplier policy and a supporting supplier and contract management information system (SCMIS).

5.5.4.2   Scope

The supplier management process should include the management of all suppliers and contracts needed to support the provision of IT services to the business.

The supplier management process should include:

- Implementation and enforcement of the supplier policy
- Maintenance of a supplier and contract management information system (SCMIS)
- Supplier and contract categorization and risk assessment
- Supplier and contract evaluation and selection
- Development, negotiation and agreement of contracts
- Contract review, renewal and termination
- Management of suppliers and supplier performance

■ Identification of improvement opportunities for inclusion in the continual service improvement (CSI) register, and the implementation of service and supplier improvement plans

■ Maintenance of standard contracts, terms and conditions

■ Management of contractual dispute resolution

■ Management of sub-contracted suppliers.

5.5.4.3 Basic concepts

Supplier categories

The supplier management process should provide a categorization scheme to categorize the suppliers and their importance to the service provider and the services provided to the business. One way to categorize the suppliers is to assess the risk and impact associated with using the supplier, and the value and importance of the supplier and its services to the business, as illustrated in Figure 5.5.

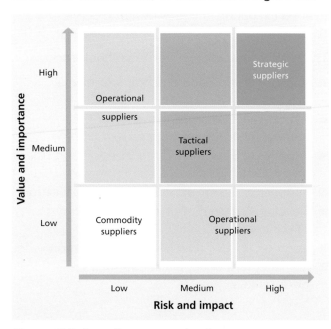

Figure 5.5 Supplier categorization

The amount of time and effort spent managing the supplier and the relationship can then be appropriate to its categorization.

5.5.5 Availability management

Availability management is the process responsible for ensuring that IT services meet the current and future availability needs of the business. Availability management defines, analyses, plans, measures and improves all aspects of the availability of IT services, and ensures that all IT infrastructures, processes, tools, roles etc. are appropriate for the agreed service level targets for availability.

5.5.5.1 Purpose and objectives

The purpose of the availability management process is to ensure that the level of availability delivered in all IT services meets the agreed availability needs and/or service level targets in a cost-effective and timely manner. Availability management is concerned with meeting both the current and future availability needs of the business.

The objectives of availability management are to:

■ Produce and maintain an appropriate and up-to-date availability plan that reflects the current and future needs of the business

■ Provide advice and guidance to all other areas of the business and IT on all availability-related issues

■ Ensure that service availability achievements meet all their agreed targets by managing services and resources-related availability performance

■ Assist with the diagnosis and resolution of availability-related incidents and problems

■ Assess the impact of all changes on the availability plan and the availability of all services and resources

■ Ensure that proactive measures to improve the availability of services are implemented wherever it is cost-justifiable to do so.

5.5.5.2 Scope

The scope of the availability management process covers the design, implementation, measurement, management and improvement of IT service and component availability. Availability management commences as soon as the availability requirements for an IT service are clear enough to be articulated. It is an ongoing process, finishing only when the IT service is decommissioned or retired.

The availability management process includes two key elements:

■ **Reactive activities** These involve the monitoring, measuring, analysis and management of all events, incidents and problems involving unavailability. These activities are principally performed as part of the operational roles.

■ **Proactive activities** These involve the proactive planning, design and improvement of availability. These activities are principally performed as part of the design and planning roles.

The availability management process should include:

■ Monitoring of all aspects of availability, reliability and maintainability of IT services and the supporting components, including appropriate events, alarms and escalation, with automated scripts for recovery

■ Maintaining a set of methods, techniques and calculations for all availability measurements, metrics and reporting

■ Actively participating in risk assessment and management activities

■ Collecting measurements and the analysis and production of regular and ad hoc reports on service and component availability

■ Understanding the agreed current and future demands of the business for IT services and their availability

■ Influencing the design of services and components to align with business availability needs

■ Producing an availability plan that enables the service provider to continue to provide and improve services in line with availability targets defined in service level agreements, and to plan and forecast future availability levels required, as specified in service level requirements

■ Maintaining a schedule of tests for all resilience and fail-over components and mechanisms

■ Assisting with the identification and resolution of any incidents and problems associated with service or component unavailability

■ Proactively improving service or component availability wherever it is cost-justifiable and meets the needs of the business.

5.5.5.3 Basic concepts

Service and component availability

Availability management is completed at two inter-connected levels:

■ **Service availability** This involves all aspects of availability and unavailability of the service and the impact of component availability on availability of the service.

■ **Component availability** This involves all aspects of availability and unavailability of components.

Availability

> **Definition**
>
> **Availability** is the ability of an IT service or other configuration item (CI) to perform its agreed function when required. Availability is determined by reliability, maintainability, serviceability, performance and security.

Availability is usually calculated as a percentage. This calculation is often based on agreed service time and downtime. It is best practice to calculate availability of an IT service using measurements of the business output.

Reliability

> **Definition**
>
> **Reliability** is a measure of how long an IT service or other configuration item (CI) can perform its agreed function without interruption.

The reliability of the service can be improved by increasing the reliability of individual components or by increasing the resilience of the service to individual component failure (increasing the component redundancy, e.g. by using load-balancing techniques).

It is often measured and reported as mean time between service incidents (MTBSI) or mean time between failures (MTBF).

Maintainability

> **Definition**
>
> **Maintainability** is a measure of how quickly and effectively an IT service or other configuration item (CI) can be restored to normal working after a failure.

Maintainability is measured and reported as mean time to restore service (MTRS).

Serviceability

> **Definition**
>
> **Serviceability** is the ability of a third-party supplier to meet the terms of its contract. Often this contract will include agreed levels of availability, reliability and/or maintainability for a supporting service or other configuration item (CI).

Vital business function

> **Definition**
>
> A **vital business function (VBF)** is a part of a business process that is critical to the success of the business. Vital business functions are an important consideration of business continuity management, IT service continuity management and availability management.

The more vital the business function generally, the greater the level of resilience and availability that needs to be incorporated into the design required in the supporting IT services.

Certain vital business functions may need special designs, which are now being used as a matter of course within service design plans, incorporating:

- **High availability** A characteristic of the IT service that minimizes or masks the effects of IT component failure to the users of a service.
- **Fault tolerance** The ability of an IT service, component or configuration item (CI) to continue to operate correctly after failure of a component part.

- **Continuous operation** An approach or design to eliminate planned downtime of an IT service. Note that individual components or configuration items may be down even though the IT service remains available.
- **Continuous availability** An approach or design to achieve 100% availability. A continuously available IT service has no planned or unplanned downtime.

5.5.6 Capacity management

Capacity management is the process responsible for ensuring that the capacity of IT services and the IT infrastructure is able to meet agreed capacity- and performance-related requirements. Capacity management includes three sub-processes: business capacity management, service capacity management, and component capacity management.

Case study: service management in practice (Brigitte's experience)

Brigitte decides to take a walk and approaches the reception desk to leave her key. In front of her a man is asking for a room for one night but he does not have a reservation. Regrettably the receptionist can't offer any vacant rooms.

As Brigitte plans to come back to Switzerland next month she wants to ensure that she will be able to stay at the hotel. Consequently, she asks the receptionist if there is cause for concern.

The receptionist replies: 'If you make a reservation a few days ahead there's usually no problem. It is only a few weeks a year where we have to turn customers away from the hotel.'

'Why don't you expand the hotel then?'

'Because the occupancy until now hasn't been high enough to justify the investment. But based on the trend over the last five years and the town plans for expanding the nearby industrial area, the hotel has now planned for a new wing with rooms to be ready in two years from now. The construction will start in a few months' time.'

5.5.6.1 Purpose and objectives

The purpose of the capacity management process is to ensure that the capacity of IT services and the IT infrastructure meets the agreed capacity- and performance-related requirements in a cost-effective and timely manner. Capacity management is concerned with meeting both the current and future capacity and performance needs of the business.

The objectives of capacity management are to:

- Produce and maintain an appropriate and up-to-date capacity plan, which reflects the current and future needs of the business
- Provide advice and guidance to all other areas of the business and IT on all capacity- and performance-related issues
- Ensure that service performance achievements meet all of their agreed targets by managing the performance and capacity of both services and resources
- Assist with the diagnosis and resolution of performance- and capacity-related incidents and problems
- Assess the impact of all changes on the capacity plan, and on the performance and capacity of all services and resources
- Ensure that proactive measures to improve the performance of services are implemented wherever it is cost-justifiable to do so.

5.5.6.2 Scope

Capacity management considers all resources required to deliver the IT service, and plans for short-, medium- and long-term business requirements. The process should encompass all areas of technology, both hardware and software, for all IT technology components and environments. Capacity management should also consider space planning and environmental systems capacity.

The capacity management process should include:

■ Monitoring patterns of business activity through performance, utilization and throughput of IT services and the supporting infrastructure, environmental, data and applications components and the production of regular and ad hoc reports on service and component capacity and performance

■ Undertaking tuning activities to make the most efficient use of existing IT resources

■ Understanding the agreed current and future demands being made by the customer for IT resources, and producing forecasts for future requirements

■ Influencing demand in conjunction with the financial management for IT services and demand management processes

■ Producing a capacity plan that enables the service provider to continue to provide services of the quality defined in SLAs, and ensuring that the plan covers a sufficient planning timeframe to meet future service levels required as defined in the service portfolio and service level requirements

■ Assisting with the identification and resolution of any incidents and problems associated with service or component capacity or performance

■ Improving proactively service or component performance, wherever it is cost-justifiable and meets the needs of the business.

5.5.6.3 Basic concepts

Business, service and component capacity management

Capacity management is a technical complex and demanding process, and in order to achieve results, it requires three supporting sub-processes:

■ The **business capacity management** sub-process translates business needs and plans into requirements for service and IT infrastructure.

■ The **service capacity management** sub-process focuses on the management, control and prediction of the end-to-end performance and capacity of the operational IT services and their workloads.

■ The **component capacity management** sub-process focuses on the management, control and prediction of the performance, utilization and capacity of individual IT technology components.

Capacity plan

One of the key activities of capacity management is to produce a plan that documents the current levels of resource utilization and service performance and forecasts the future requirements for new resources to support the IT services that underpin the business activities.

A **capacity plan** is used to manage the resources required to deliver IT services. The plan contains details of current and historic usage of IT services and components, and any issues that need to be addressed (including related improvement activities). The plan also contains scenarios for different predictions of business demand, and costed options to deliver the agreed service level targets.

The production and maintenance of a capacity plan should occur at predefined intervals. It is, essentially, an investment plan and should therefore be published annually, in line with the business or budget lifecycle, and completed before the start of negotiations on future budgets.

5.5.7 IT service continuity management

IT service continuity management is the process responsible for managing risks that could seriously affect IT services. IT service continuity management ensures that the IT service provider can always provide minimum agreed service levels, by reducing the risk to an acceptable level and planning for the recovery of IT services. IT service continuity management supports business continuity management.

Case study: service management in practice (Brigitte's experience)

Brigitte notices that the receptionist seems sad and asks him if he is all right. He hesitates before he answers. He tells her that one of his good friends, a waiter at another hotel, has just lost his job. The hotel was struck by a disaster – an avalanche destroyed most of the hotel. The disaster was managed very badly and no one seemed to be prepared for a situation like this.

For example, there hadn't been any plan for re-housing the guests. As a result the customers had lost confidence in the hotel and after a short while the hotel went bankrupt, even though the insurance had covered the reconstruction of the hotel.

5.5.7.1 Purpose and objectives

The purpose of the IT service continuity management process is to support the overall business continuity management (BCM) process by ensuring that, by managing the risks that could seriously affect IT services, the IT service provider can always provide minimum agreed business continuity-related service levels.

The objectives of IT service continuity management are to:

- Produce and maintain a set of IT service continuity plans that support the overall business continuity plans of the organization
- Complete regular business impact assessment exercises to ensure that all continuity plans are maintained in line with changing business impacts and requirements
- Conduct regular risk assessment and management exercises to manage IT services within an agreed level of business risk, in conjunction with the business and the availability management and information security management processes
- Provide advice and guidance to all other areas of the business and IT on all continuity-related issues
- Ensure that appropriate continuity mechanisms are put in place to meet or exceed the agreed business continuity targets

- Assess the impact of all changes on the IT service continuity plans and supporting methods and procedures
- Ensure that proactive measures to improve the availability of services are implemented wherever it is cost-justifiable to do so
- Negotiate and agree contracts with suppliers for the provision of the necessary recovery capability to support all continuity plans in conjunction with the supplier management process.

5.5.7.2 Scope

IT service continuity management focuses on those events that the business considers significant enough to be treated as a 'disaster'. Less significant events will be dealt with as part of the incident management process.

IT service continuity management primarily considers the IT assets and configurations that support the business processes, not items such as office and personal accommodation. Furthermore, IT service continuity management does not usually directly cover longer-term risks such as those from changes in business direction, diversification, restructuring, major competitor failure and so on.

The IT service continuity management process includes:

- The agreement of the scope of the IT service continuity management process and the policies adopted
- Business impact analysis (BIA) to quantify the impact that loss of the IT service would have on the business
- Risk assessment and management
- Production of an overall IT service continuity management strategy, which must be integrated into the business continuity management strategy

- Production of an IT service continuity management plan, which again must be integrated with the overall business continuity management plans
- Testing of the plans
- Ongoing operation and maintenance of the plans.

5.5.7.3 Basic concepts

Business impact analysis

The purpose of a business impact analysis (BIA) is to quantify the impact to the business that loss of service would have. This impact could be a 'hard' impact that can be precisely identified – such as financial loss – or a 'soft' impact – such as public relations, morale, health and safety or loss of competitive advantage. The BIA will identify the most important services to the organization and will therefore be a key input to the strategy.

> **Definition**
>
> **Business impact analysis** (BIA) is the activity in business continuity management that identifies vital business functions and their dependencies. These dependencies may include suppliers, people, other business processes, IT services etc.

Business impact analysis defines the recovery requirements for IT services. These requirements include recovery time objectives (RTOs), recovery point objectives (RPOs) and minimum service level targets for each IT service.

Risk assessment

The second driver in determining IT service continuity management requirements is the likelihood that a disaster or other serious service disruption will actually occur. This is an assessment of the level of threat and the extent to which an organization is vulnerable to that threat. Risk assessment can also be used in assessing and reducing the chance of normal operational incidents and is a technique used by availability management to ensure that the required availability and reliability levels can be maintained.

Definition

Risk assessment covers the initial steps of risk management: analysing the value of assets to the business, identifying threats to those assets, and evaluating how vulnerable each asset is to those threats. Risk assessment can be quantitative (based on numerical data) or qualitative.

Risk management is concerned with identifying appropriate risk responses or cost-justifiable countermeasures to combat the risks identified by risk assessment. A standard methodology, such as Management of Risk (M_o_R®), should be used to assess and manage risks within an organization.

5.5.8 Information security management

Information security management is the process responsible for ensuring that the confidentiality, integrity and availability of an organization's assets, information, data and IT services match the agreed needs of the business. Information security management supports business security and has a wider scope than that of the IT service provider, and includes handling of paper, building access, phone calls etc. for the entire organization.

Case study: service management in practice (Brigitte's experience)

Brigitte meets the hotel manager in the lobby and they continue their little chat on the installation of the electronic card key system. She wonders why a peaceful little hotel in the Alps is installing a card key system.

He takes a deep breath before he answers, but as she promises not to tell anyone he continues: 'There have been a number of thefts from the hotel, mainly cigarettes from the restaurant but also other objects. As a result the management evaluated the overall hotel security and made a plan for improvements. Based on the plan, a security policy was developed and the management team have committed to ensure that it is implemented within a reasonable timeframe. A part of the implementation is to restrict the physical access to the hotel.'

The manager expresses his hope that the increased physical security together with some of the other measures in the security policy will eliminate the thefts. He therefore looks forward to evaluating the results of the initiatives in six months.

5.5.8.1 Purpose and objectives

The purpose of the information security management process is to align IT security with business security and ensure that the confidentiality, integrity and availability of the organization's assets, information, data and IT services always match the agreed needs of the business.

The objective of information security management is to protect the interests of those relying on information, and the systems and communications that deliver the information, from harm resulting from failures of confidentiality, integrity and availability.

For most organizations, the security objective is met when:

■ Information is observed by or disclosed to only those who have a right to know (confidentiality).
■ Information is complete, accurate and protected against unauthorized modification (integrity).
■ Information is available and usable when required, and the systems that provide it can appropriately resist attacks and recover from or prevent failures (availability).
■ Business transactions, as well as information exchanges between enterprises, or with partners, can be trusted (authenticity and non-repudiation).

5.5.8.2 Scope

The information security management process should be the focal point for all IT security issues, and must ensure that an information security policy is produced, maintained and enforced that covers the use and misuse of all IT systems and services.

Information security management needs to understand the total IT and business security environment, including the:

■ Business security policy and plans
■ Current business operation and its security requirements
■ Future business plans and requirements

■ Legislative and regulatory requirements
■ Obligations and responsibilities with regard to security contained within SLAs
■ The business and IT risks and their management.

The information security management process should include:

■ The production, maintenance, distribution and enforcement of an information security policy and supporting security policies
■ Understanding the agreed current and future security requirements of the business and the existing business security policy and plans
■ Implementation of a set of security controls that support the information security policy and manage risks associated with access to services, information and systems
■ Documentation of all security controls, together with the operation and maintenance of the controls and their associated risks
■ Management of suppliers and contracts regarding access to systems and services, in conjunction with supplier management
■ Management of all security breaches, incidents and problems associated with all systems and services
■ The proactive improvement of security controls and security risk management, and the reduction of security risks
■ Integration of security aspects within all other IT service management processes.

5.5.8.3 Basic concepts

Information security policy

Information security management activities should be focused on and driven by an overall information security policy and a set of underpinning specific policies. The policy should cover all areas of security, be appropriate and meet the needs of the business and should include:

- An overall information security policy
- A policy on the use and misuse of IT assets
- An access control policy
- A password control policy
- An email policy
- An internet policy
- An antivirus policy
- An information classification policy
- A document classification policy
- A remote access policy
- A policy with regard to supplier access to IT service, information and components

- A copyright infringement policy for electronic material
- An asset disposal policy
- A records retention policy.

In most cases, the security policies should be widely available to all customers and users, and their compliance should be referred to in all service level requirements, SLAs, contracts and agreements. The policies should be authorized by top executive management within the business and IT, and compliance with them should be endorsed regularly. All security policies should be reviewed – and, where necessary, revised – at least annually.

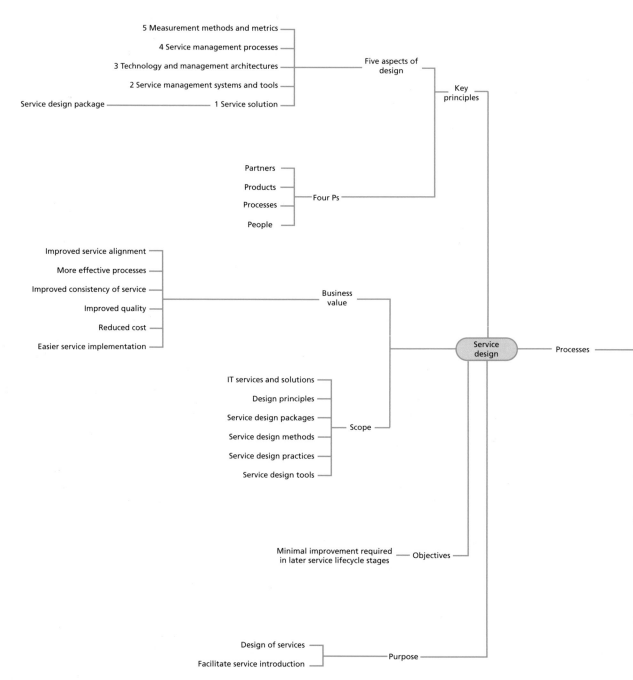

Figure 5.6 Overview of Chapter 5

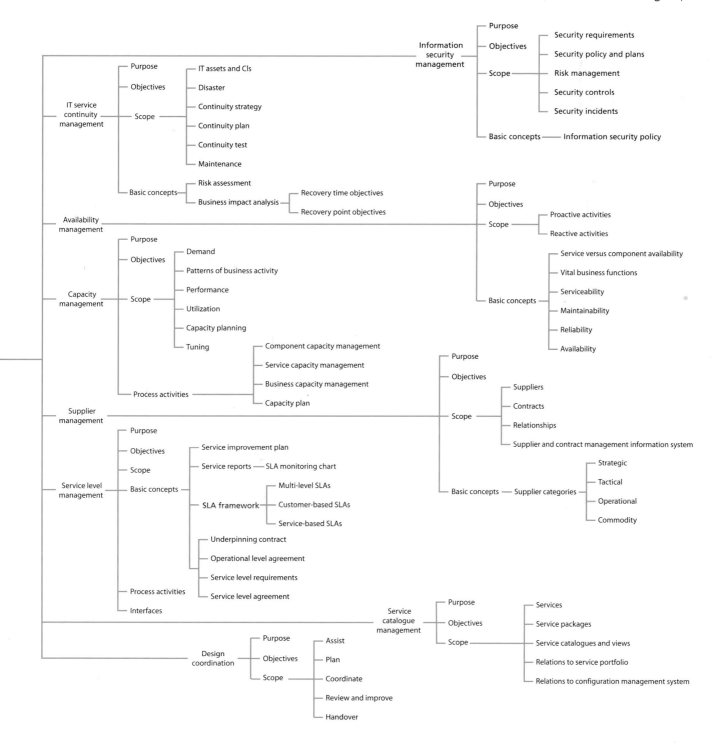

5.6 SAMPLE QUESTIONS

1 Which of the following is NOT an objective of service design?

   a To design services to realize the service provider's strategy

   b To design the organizational structure for the operation of a high-quality service

   c To design the measurement methods and metrics in order to assess the effectiveness of service design

   d To design efficient and effective processes for the design, transition, operation and improvement of high-quality IT services

2 Which of the following is the BEST description of a service level agreement?

   a The organization supplying services to one or more internal customers or external customers

   b An agreement between a service provider and the customers of the service which details the services, their targets and the responsibilities of both parties

   c An underpinning agreement between an IT service provider and another part of the same organization that assists with the provision of services

   d An agreement between a service provider and project teams which details the intended delivery of projects into service

3 Which of the following is NOT one of the aspects of service design?

   a The partners responsible for the service design

   b The technology and management architecture

   c The measurement methods and metrics

   d The processes required

4 Which process controls all activities and processes during service design?

   a Transition planning

   b Service level management

   c Risk management

   d Design coordination

5 Which of the following terms is often used to describe reliability?

   a Mean time between service incidents (MTBSI)

   b Mean time to restore service (MTRS)

   c Downtime

   d Serviceability

Service transition

6

6 Service transition

Service transition packages, builds, tests, evaluates, deploys, transfers or retires new or changed services or service components. In addition, service transition manages knowledge, information and data required by the service provider, and it manages risks relating to service transition.

Case study: Service management in practice (Brigitte's experience)

As the planning and design of the new conference services progress, the project manager has started thinking about the implementation phase. He has already drafted some activities that he expects to include in the transition phase:

- Plan the implementation in detail
- Assemble and build the designed facilities
- Train the staff in the facilities and processes
- Test that the conference facilities function as they are intended to
- Inspect that the facilities conform to the requirements of local businesses as well as regulations put forward by the local authorities.

6.1 PURPOSE AND OBJECTIVES

The purpose of the service transition stage is to ensure that new, modified or retired services meet the expectations of the business as documented in the service strategy and service design stages of the lifecycle.

The main objectives of service transition are to:

- Plan and manage service changes efficiently and effectively
- Manage risks relating to new, changed or retired services
- Successfully deploy service releases into supported environments
- Set correct expectations on the performance and use of new or changed services
- Ensure that service changes create the expected business value
- Provide good-quality knowledge and information about services and service assets.

6.2 SCOPE

Service transition covers transition of new and changed services into supported environments, including release, planning, building, testing, evaluation and deployment. Service transition also covers retirement and transfer of services between service providers.

The following processes are within the scope of service transition:

- Transition planning and support
- Change management
- Service asset and configuration management
- Release and deployment management
- Service validation and testing
- Change evaluation
- Knowledge management.

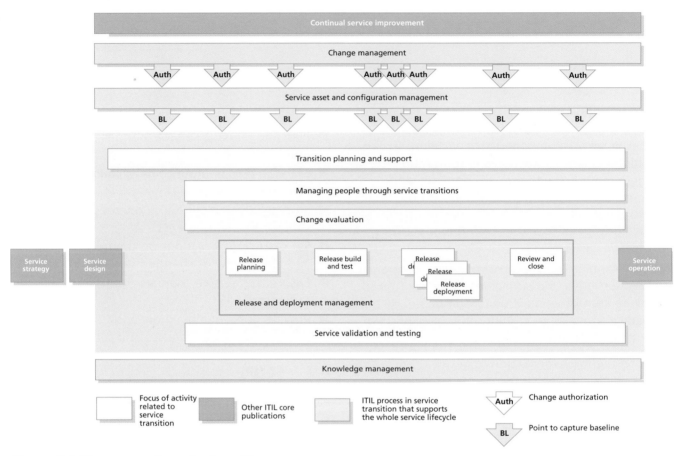

Figure 6.1 The scope of service transition

Figure 6.1 shows all the processes within the scope of the service transition stage. Processes that are largely within the service transition stage of the service lifecycle are shown within the central rectangle; the other stages of the service lifecycle that come before and after these processes are shown in the smaller darker rectangles.

The following lifecycle processes described in the service transition stage support all lifecycle stages:

■ Change management
■ Service asset and configuration management (SACM)
■ Knowledge management.

6.3   BUSINESS VALUE

Adopting and implementing consistent approaches for service transition will:

- Enable projects to estimate the cost, timing, resource requirement and risks associated with the service transition stage more accurately
- Result in higher volumes of successful change
- Enable service transition assets to be shared and re-used across projects and services
- Reduce delays from unexpected clashes and dependencies – for example, if multiple projects need to use the same test environment at the same time
- Increase confidence that the new or changed service can be delivered to specification without unexpectedly affecting other services or stakeholders.

6.4   KEY PRINCIPLES

6.4.1   Release policy

Formal policies for service transition should be defined, documented and approved, including a release policy. The release policy should be defined for one or more services and (among other things) include:

- The unique identification, numbering and naming conventions for different types of release, together with a description
- The roles and responsibilities at each stage in the release and deployment management process
- The requirement to only use software assets from the definitive media library (see section 6.5.2.3)
- The expected frequency for each type of release

- The approach for accepting and grouping changes into a release, e.g. how enhancements are prioritized for inclusion
- The mechanism to automate the build, installation and release distribution processes to improve re-use, repeatability and efficiency
- Details of how the configuration baseline for the release is captured and verified against the actual release contents
- Exit and entry criteria and authority for acceptance of the release into each service transition stage and into the controlled test, training, disaster recovery and production environments
- Criteria and authorization to exit early-life support and handover to the service operation functions.

6.5   PROCESSES

The ITIL Foundation syllabus covers the following service transition processes:

- Transition planning and support
- Service asset and configuration management (SACM)
- Change management
- Release and deployment management
- Knowledge management.

6.5.1   Transition planning and support

Transition planning and support is the process responsible for planning all service transition processes and coordinating the required resources.

6.5.1.1 Purpose and objectives

The purpose of the transition planning and support process is to provide overall planning for service transitions and to coordinate the resources that they require.

The objectives of transition planning and support are to:

- Plan and coordinate the resources to ensure that the requirements of service strategy encoded in service design are effectively realized in service operation.
- Coordinate activities across projects, suppliers and service teams where required.
- Establish new or changed services into supported environments within the predicted cost, quality and time estimates.
- Establish new or modified management information systems and tools, technology and management architectures, service management processes, and measurement methods and metrics to meet requirements established during the service design stage of the lifecycle.
- Ensure that all parties adopt the common framework of standard processes and supporting systems.
- Provide clear and comprehensive plans that enable customer and business change projects to align their activities with the service transition plans.
- Identify, manage and control risks, to minimize the chance of failure and disruption across transition activities.
- Monitor and improve the performance of the service transition lifecycle stage.

6.5.1.2 Scope

The scope of transition planning and support includes:

- Maintaining policies, standards and models for service transition activities and processes
- Guiding each major change or new service through all the service transition processes
- Coordinating the efforts needed to enable multiple transitions to be managed at the same time
- Prioritizing conflicting requirements for service transition resources
- Planning the budget and resources needed to fulfil future requirements for service transition
- Reviewing and improving the performance of transition planning and support activities
- Ensuring that service transition is coordinated with programme and project management, service design and service development activities.

Transition planning and support is not responsible for detailed planning of the build, test and deployment of individual changes or releases; these activities are carried out as part of change management and release and deployment management.

6.5.2 Service asset and configuration management

Service asset and configuration management (SACM) is the process responsible for managing assets vital to running the customer's or organization's business.

6.5.2.1 Purpose and objectives

The purpose of the service asset and configuration management process is to ensure that the assets required to deliver services are properly controlled, and that accurate and reliable information about those assets is available when and where it is needed. This information includes details of how the assets have been configured and the relationships between assets.

The objectives of service asset and configuration management are to:

- Ensure that assets under the control of the IT organization are identified, controlled and properly cared for throughout their lifecycle.
- Identify, control, record, report, audit and verify services and other configuration items (CIs) including versions, baselines, constituent components, their attributes and relationships.
- Account for, manage and protect the integrity of CIs through the service lifecycle by working with change management to ensure that only authorized components are used and only authorized changes are made.
- Ensure the integrity of CIs and configurations required to control the services by establishing and maintaining an accurate and complete configuration management system (CMS).
- Maintain accurate configuration information on the historical, planned and current state of services and other CIs.
- Support efficient and effective service management processes by providing accurate configuration information to enable people to make decisions at the right time.

6.5.2.2 Scope

The scope of service asset and configuration management (SACM) includes management of the complete lifecycle of every configuration item (CI), including interfaces to internal and external service providers where there are assets and configuration items that need to be controlled, e.g. shared assets.

6.5.2.3 Basic concepts

Configuration item

Service assets that need to be managed in order to deliver services are known as configuration items (CIs). Other service assets may be required to deliver the service, but if they cannot be individually managed then they are not configuration items. Every CI is a service asset, but many service assets are not CIs.

> **Definition**
>
> A **configuration item** (CI) is any component or other service asset that needs to be managed in order to deliver an IT service.

Information about each configuration item is recorded in a configuration record within the configuration management system (CMS) and is maintained throughout its lifecycle by service asset and configuration management.

Configuration items are under the control of change management. They typically include IT services, hardware, software, buildings, people and formal documentation such as process documentation and service level agreements.

There will be a variety of CIs. The following example categories may help to identify them:

- **Service lifecycle CIs** The business case, service management plans, service lifecycle plans, service design package, release and change plans and test plans
- **Service CIs** Service capability assets (management, organization, processes, knowledge, people), service resource assets (financial capital, systems, applications, information, data, infrastructure and facilities, financial capital, people), service model, service

package, release package and service acceptance criteria

- **Organization CIs** An organization's business strategy or other policies
- **Internal CIs** Those delivered by individual projects, including assets such as hardware and software that are required to deliver and maintain the service and infrastructure

- **External CIs** External customer requirements and agreements, releases from suppliers or sub-contractors, and external services
- **Interface CIs** Escalation documents and interface agreements.

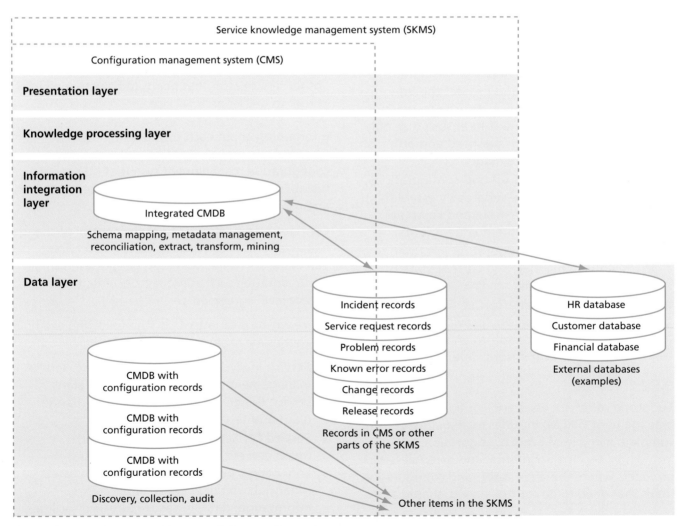

Figure 6.2 Architectural layers of the configuration management system

Configuration management system

> **Definition**
>
> A **configuration management system** (CMS) is a set of tools, data and information that is used to support service asset and configuration management.

The CMS includes tools for collecting, storing, managing, updating, analysing and presenting data about all configuration items and their relationships. The CMS may also include information about incidents, problems, known errors, changes and releases.

The CMS is maintained by service asset and configuration management and is used by all IT service management processes.

The CMS maintains the relationships between all service components and any related incidents and problems, known errors, and change and releases. The CMS may also link to corporate data about employees, suppliers, locations and business units, customers and users.

The CMS is part of a service knowledge management system (SKMS) that includes data, information integration, knowledge processing and presentation layers. Figure 6.2 shows the architectural layers of the configuration management system.

The presentation layer of the CMS will contain views and dashboards that are required by people who need access to configuration information.

The CMS typically contains configuration data and information that combines into an integrated set of views for different stakeholders through the service lifecycle

At the data level, the CMS may include data from configuration records stored in several physical configuration management databases (CMDBs), which come together at the information integration layer to form an integrated CMDB. The integrated CMDB may also incorporate information from external data sources such as an HR database or financial database. The CMS will provide access to this external data wherever possible rather than duplicating data.

> **Case study: service management in practice (Brigitte's experience)**
>
> Later that evening in the restaurant, Brigitte overhears a conversation between the hotel manager and the chef. The manager is dissatisfied with the fact that the chef doesn't take his administrative duties seriously enough. The chef has just introduced a new menu card without recording it. It turns out that the hotel maintains a database of all relevant equipment, people, suppliers and processes that are used to provide the services. The staff are supposed to register selected assets such as rooms, beds and restaurant tables and the impact of these items on the services and the guests in the database every time they make a change to an item.
>
> Over the years, the hotel has gained much experience in which data (such as equipment, people, suppliers and processes) it is important to register and maintain. Currently the configuration database includes information about:
>
> ■ Guests
> ■ Staff members
> ■ Guest rooms
> ■ Beds
> ■ Meeting rooms

- Conference equipment
- Restaurant tables
- Menu cards
- Suppliers
- IT applications
- Processes
- Functions (reception, kitchen etc.)
- Reservations of rooms (relations between rooms and guests) – it is possible to identify the vacant and reserved rooms and to see which rooms a guest stayed in during previous visits
- Reservation of tables (relations between tables and guests)
- Ownership and responsibility (relations between staff members and other items)
- Allocation of staff (relations between staff members and functions or roles).

This information makes it possible to manage the provided services and analyse the impact of faults or changes to underpinning items.

Definitive media library

The definitive media library (DML) should include definitive copies of purchased software (along with licence documents or information) as well as software developed on site. Master copies of controlled documentation for a system are also stored in the definitive media library in electronic form.

The definitive media library will also include a physical store to hold master copies, e.g. a fireproof safe.

The definitive media library is a single logical storage area even if there are multiple locations.

All software in the definitive media library is under the control of change management and is recorded in the CMS (see Figure 6.3), strictly controlled by service asset and configuration management (SACM).

6.5.3 Change management

Change management is the process responsible for controlling changes to deliver early realization of benefits with minimum risk and adverse impact.

Case study: service management in practice (Brigitte's experience)

The very first time Brigitte stayed at the hotel no internet connection was available for the guests. Brigitte had been quite surprised as the majority of the hotel guests were business people like herself. Upon her departure she had told the receptionist that she had missed that service and the receptionist had made a note of her request and told her that she had just received the same request from one of their travel agency customers.

To Brigitte's surprise she got a call from the hotel when she came home; the person who called told her that he was assessing and evaluating her suggestion for an internet connection.

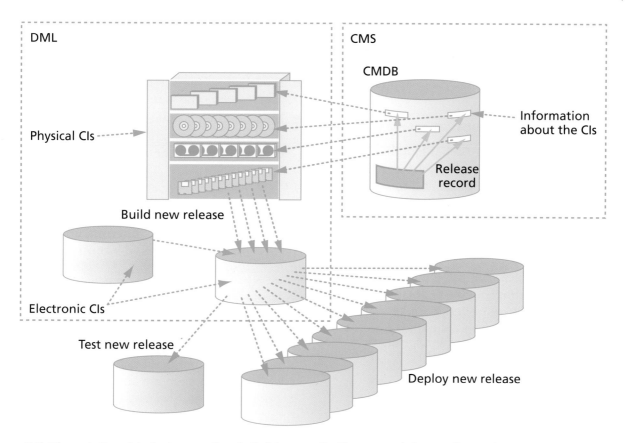

Figure 6.3 The relationship between the definitive media library and the configuration management system

He had been talking to a number of people, including technicians to assess the possible technical solutions and the financial manager to raise funding. Now he wanted to listen to a potential customer's viewpoint. He asked her some questions on the reason for her request and whether she as a guest would be willing to pay for the service.

When she came back to the hotel a year later there was a wireless internet connection in her room. She only had to buy an access code at the reception.

And once more she received – again to her surprise – a call from the hotel when she came home; this time they wanted to know whether the internet connection met her expectations or whether anything needed to be changed from Brigitte's perspective.

6.5.3.1 Purpose and objectives

The purpose of the change management process is to control the lifecycle of all changes, enabling beneficial changes to be made with minimum disruption to IT services.

The objectives of change management are to:

- Respond to the customer's changing business requirements while maximizing value and reducing incidents, disruption and re-work.
- Respond to the business and IT requests for change that will align the services with the business needs.
- Ensure that changes are recorded and evaluated, and that authorized changes are prioritized, planned, tested, implemented, documented and reviewed in a controlled manner.
- Ensure that all changes to configuration items are recorded in the configuration management system.
- Optimize overall business risk – it is often correct to minimize business risk, but sometimes it is appropriate to knowingly accept a risk because of the potential benefit.

6.5.3.2 Scope

The scope of service transition covers any addition, modification or removal of anything that could have an effect on IT services. The scope should include changes to all architectures, processes, tools, metrics and documentation, as well as changes to IT services and other configuration items.

The scope also covers all changes to any of the five aspects of service design:

- Service solutions for new or changed services, including all of the functional requirements, resources and capabilities needed and agreed

- Management information systems and tools
- Technology architectures and management architectures required to provide the services
- Processes needed to design, transition, operate and improve the services
- Measurement systems, methods and metrics for the services, the architectures, their constituent components and the processes.

6.5.3.3 Basic concepts

Change, request for change and change record

The terms 'change', 'change record' and 'request for change' (RFC) are often used inconsistently, leading to confusion.

> **Definitions**
>
> A **change** is the addition, modification or removal of anything that could have an effect on IT services.
>
> A **request for change** (RFC) is a formal proposal for a change to be made. It includes details of the proposed change, and may be recorded on paper or electronically. The term RFC is often misused to mean a change record, or the change itself.
>
> A **change record** contains the details of a change. Each change record documents the lifecycle of a single change. A change record is created for every request for change that is received, even those that are subsequently rejected. Change records should reference the configuration items that are affected by the change. Change records may be stored in the configuration management system or elsewhere in the service knowledge management system.

RFCs are only used to submit requests; they are not used to communicate the decisions of change management or to document the details of the change. A change record contains all the required information about a change, including information from the RFC, and is used to manage the lifecycle of that change.

Change types

For different change types there are often specific procedures, e.g. for impact assessment and change authorization. There are three different types of service change:

- **Normal change** Normal changes go through the full assessment, authorization and implementation stages. Normal changes are typically categorized as major, significant or minor.
- **Standard change** A standard change is a pre-approved change that is low risk, relatively common and follows a procedure or work instruction – for example, a password reset or provision of standard equipment to a new employee. Every standard change should have a change model that defines the steps to follow, including how the change should be logged and managed as well as how it should be implemented. The crucial elements of a standard change are as follows:
  - There is a defined trigger to initiate the change, for example a service request or an exception generated by event management.
  - The tasks are well known, documented and proven.
  - Authority is effectively given in advance.
  - Budgetary approval will typically be preordained or within the control of the change requester.
  - The risk is usually low and always well-understood.

- **Emergency change** Emergency change is reserved only for highly critical changes that must be implemented as soon as possible, for example to resolve a major incident or implement a security patch.

  Emergency changes are sometimes required and should be designed carefully and tested as much as possible before use, otherwise the impact of the emergency change may be greater than the original incident. Details of emergency changes may be documented retrospectively.

  In an emergency situation it may not be possible to convene a full change advisory board (CAB) meeting. Where CAB approval is required, this will be provided by the emergency CAB (ECAB).

Change proposals

Major changes that involve significant cost, risk or organizational impact will usually be initiated through the service portfolio management process. Before the new or changed service is chartered, it is important that the change is reviewed for its potential impact on other services, on shared resources and on the change schedule.

Change proposals are submitted to change management before chartering new or changed services in order to ensure that potential conflicts for resources or other issues are identified. Authorization of the change proposal does not authorize implementation of the change but simply allows the service to be chartered so that service design activity can commence.

The change proposal is normally created by the service portfolio management process and is passed to change management for authorization. In some organizations, change proposals may be created by a programme management office or by individual projects. The change proposal should include:

- A high-level description of the new, changed or retired service, including business outcomes to be supported, and utility and warranty to be provided
- A full business case including risks, issues and alternatives, as well as budget and financial expectations
- An outline schedule for design and implementation of the change.

After the new or changed service is chartered, RFCs will be used in the normal way to request authorization for specific changes. These RFCs will be associated with the change proposal so that change management has a view of the overall strategic intent and can prioritize and review these RFCs appropriately.

Change models

Organizations will find it helpful to predefine change models – and apply them to appropriate changes when they occur. A change model is a way of predefining the steps that should be taken to handle a particular type of change in an agreed way.

The change model includes:

- The steps that should be taken to handle the change, including handling issues and unexpected events
- The chronological order these steps should be taken in, with any dependences or co-processing defined
- Responsibilities: who should do what
- Timescales and thresholds for completion of the actions
- Escalation procedures: who should be contacted and when.

Remediation planning

No change should be approved without having explicitly addressed the question of what to do if it is not successful. Ideally, there will be a back-out plan, which will restore the organization to its initial situation, often through the reloading of a baselined set of configuration items (CIs) – especially software and data. However, not all changes are reversible, in which case an alternative approach to remediation is required.

Change advisory board

The change advisory board (CAB) is a body that exists to support the authorization of changes and to assist change management in the assessment, prioritization and scheduling of changes.

As and when a CAB is convened, members should be chosen who are capable of ensuring that all changes within the scope of the CAB are adequately assessed from both a business and a technical viewpoint.

To achieve this, the CAB needs to include people with a clear understanding across the whole range of stakeholder needs. The change manager will normally chair the CAB, and potential members include:

- Customer(s)
- User manager(s)
- User group representative(s)
- Business relationship managers
- Service owners
- Applications developers/maintainers
- Specialists/technical consultants
- Services and operations staff
- Facilities/office services staff (where changes may affect moves/accommodation and vice versa)
- Contractors' or third parties' representatives, e.g. in outsourcing situations
- Other parties as applicable to specific circumstances.

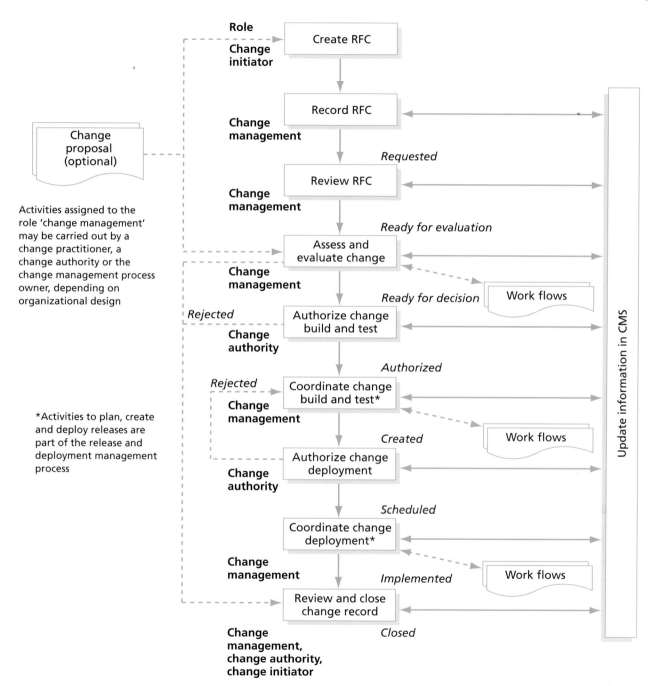

Figure 6.4 Example of a process flow for a normal change

In an emergency situation it may not be possible to convene a full CAB meeting. Where CAB authorization is required, this will be provided by the emergency change advisory board (ECAB). Change procedures should specify how the composition of the CAB and ECAB will be determined in each instance.

6.5.3.4 Process activities

Overall change management activities include:

- Planning and controlling changes
- Change and release scheduling
- Communications
- Change decision-making and change authorization
- Ensuring that there are remediation plans
- Measurement and control
- Management reporting
- Understanding the impact of change
- Continual improvement.

Typical activities in managing individual changes (see Figure 6.4) are to:

- Create and record the RFC
- Review RFCs and filter changes
- Assess and evaluate the change:
  - Establish the appropriate level of change authority
  - Establish relevant areas of interest (who should be involved in the CAB)
  - Evaluate the business justification, impact, cost, benefits, risks and predicted performance of the change
  - Request formal evaluation of the change from the change evaluation process if this is required

- Authorize the change:
  - Obtain authorization/rejection
  - Communicate the decision with all stakeholders, in particular the initiator of the RFC
- Plan updates
- Coordinate change implementation
- Review and close the change.

6.5.3.5 Interfaces

In order to be able to define clear boundaries, dependencies and rules, change management and release and deployment management should be integrated with processes used for organizational programmes or projects, supplier management and also suppliers' processes and procedures. There will be occasions when a proposed change will potentially have a wider impact on other parts of the organization (e.g. facilities or business operations), or vice versa, and the service change process must interface appropriately with other processes involved:

- **Programme and project management** Programme and project management must work in partnership with change management to align all the processes and people involved in service change initiatives.
- **Organizational and stakeholder change management** It is essential that organizational aspects of change management are properly considered and that the change management process has appropriate interfaces with the people carrying out this work.
- **Sourcing and partnering** Effective change management practices and principles should manage relationships with internal and external vendors and suppliers effectively.

- **Service portfolio management** Service portfolio management prioritizes and charters strategic changes, and some change requests require analysis by the service portfolio management process.
- **Capacity management and demand management** Capacity management should assess every change for its impact on capacity, and changes arising from capacity management should be implemented through the change management process.
- **IT service continuity management** Every change should be assessed for its impact on IT service continuity and continuity plans, and procedures should be kept under change management control.
- **Information security management** Security changes are implemented through the change management process, and every change should be assessed for its potential impact on information security.
- **Service asset and configuration management** The configuration management system (CMS) provides access to configuration information to enable impact assessment of changes and change tracking.
- **Problem management** Problem management ensures that all resolutions or workarounds that require a change to a configuration item (CI) are submitted through change management.

6.5.4 Release and deployment management

Release and deployment management is the process responsible for delivering new functionality required while protecting the integrity of existing services.

Case study: service management in practice (Brigitte's experience)

Brigitte was glad to find the new wireless internet connection service available the second time she visited the hotel. But she also wondered why she had to order a room with internet in advance and why the hotel hadn't just implemented the service in all rooms.

Jacob, who was assigned to implement the internet services, explained that the hotel had wanted to keep control of the deployment so they had chosen a phased approach, to ensure that one phase was a success before moving on to the next.

Actually the hotel started with an installation in the reception area. In the second phase the service had been available in a limited number of rooms to guests who specifically asked for it. Now in the third phase they advertised the service and they were planning to roll out the service to all remaining rooms.

6.5.4.1 Purpose and objectives

The purpose of the release and deployment management process is to plan, schedule and control the build, test and deployment of releases, and to deliver new functionality required by the business while protecting the integrity of existing services.

The objectives of release and deployment management are to:

- Define and agree release and deployment management plans with customers and stakeholders
- Create and test release packages that consist of related configuration items that are compatible with each other

■ Ensure that the integrity of a release package and its constituent components is maintained throughout the transition activities, and that all release packages are stored in a definitive media library (DML) and recorded accurately in the configuration management system (CMS)

■ Deploy release packages from the DML to the live environment following an agreed plan and schedule

■ Ensure that all release packages can be tracked, installed, tested, verified and/or uninstalled or backed out if appropriate

■ Ensure that organization and stakeholder change is managed during release and deployment activities

■ Ensure that a new or changed service and its enabling systems, technology and organization are capable of delivering the agreed utility and warranty

■ Record and manage deviations, risks and issues related to the new or changed service and take necessary corrective action

■ Ensure that skills and knowledge are transferred to customers, users and service operation functions.

6.5.4.2 Scope

The scope of release and deployment management includes the processes, systems and functions to package, build, test and deploy a release into live use and formally hand the service over to the service operation functions. The scope includes all configuration items required to implement a release, for example:

■ Physical assets such as a server or network

■ Virtual assets such as a virtual server or virtual storage

■ Applications and software

■ Training for users and IT staff

■ Services, including all related contracts and agreements.

Although release and deployment management is responsible for ensuring that appropriate testing takes place, the actual testing is carried out as part of the service validation and testing process.

6.5.4.3 Basic concept

Release

> **Definition**
>
> A **release** is a collection of one or more changes to an IT service that are built, tested and deployed together. A single release may include changes to hardware, software, documentation, processes and other components.

6.5.4.4 Process activities

There are four phases to release and deployment management (see Figure 6.5):

■ **Release and deployment planning** Plans for creating and deploying the release are created. This phase starts with change management authorization to plan a release and ends with change management authorization to create the release.

■ **Release build and test** The release package is built, tested and checked into the definitive media library (DML). This phase starts with change management authorization to build the release and ends with change management authorization for the baselined release package to be checked into the DML by service asset and configuration management. This phase only happens once for each release.

■ **Deployment** The release package in the DML is deployed to the live environment. This phase starts with change management authorization to deploy the release package to one or more target environments and ends with handover to the service operation functions and early-life support. There may be many separate deployment phases for each release, depending on the planned deployment options.

■ **Review and close** Experience and feedback are captured, performance targets and achievements are reviewed and lessons are learned.

Figure 6.5 shows multiple points where an authorized change triggers release and deployment management activity. This does not require a separate request for change (RFC) at each stage. Some organizations manage a whole release with a single change request and separate authorization at each stage for activities to continue, while other organizations require a separate RFC for each stage. Both of these approaches are acceptable; what is important is that change management authorization is received before commencing each stage.

6.5.5 Knowledge management

Knowledge management is the process responsible for sharing service perspectives, ideas, experience and information to improve service efficiency and enable informed decisions.

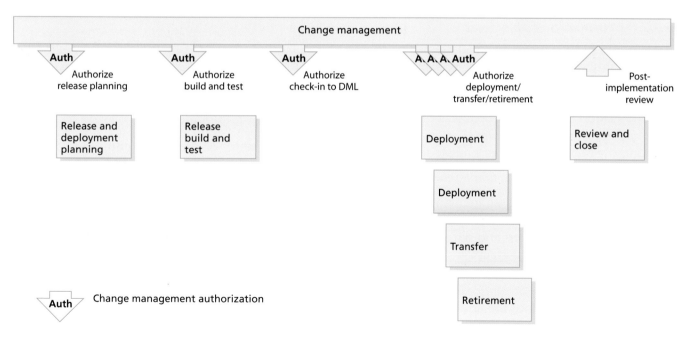

Figure 6.5 Phases of release and deployment management

6.5.5.1 Purpose and objectives

The purpose of the knowledge management process is to share perspectives, ideas, experience and information, and to ensure that these are available in the right place and at the right time. The knowledge management process enables informed decisions and improves efficiency by reducing the need to rediscover knowledge.

The objectives of knowledge management are to:

- Improve the quality of management decision-making by ensuring that reliable and secure knowledge, information and data is available throughout the service lifecycle
- Enable the service provider to be more efficient and improve quality of service, increase satisfaction and reduce the cost of service by reducing the need to rediscover knowledge
- Ensure that staff have a clear and common understanding of the value that their services provide to customers and the ways in which benefits are realized from the use of those services

- Maintain a service knowledge management system (SKMS) that provides controlled access to knowledge, information and data that is appropriate for each audience
- Gather, analyse, store, share, use and maintain knowledge, information and data throughout the service provider organization.

6.5.5.2 Scope

Knowledge management is a whole lifecycle-wide process in that it is relevant to all lifecycle stages and hence is referenced throughout ITIL from the perspective of each publication. Knowledge management includes oversight of the management of knowledge, the information and data from which that knowledge derives.

6.5.5.3 Basic concepts

Data to information to knowledge to wisdom

Knowledge management is typically displayed within the data-to-information-to-knowledge-to-wisdom (DIKW) structure (see Figure 6.6). The use of these terms is set out below:

- **Data** is a set of discrete facts about events. Most organizations capture significant amounts of data in highly structured databases such as service management and service asset and configuration management tools/systems and databases.
- **Information** comes from providing context to data. Information is typically stored in semi-structured content such as documents, email and multimedia.
- **Knowledge** is composed of the tacit experiences, ideas, insights, values and judgements of individuals. People gain knowledge both from their own and from their peers' expertise, as well as from the analysis of

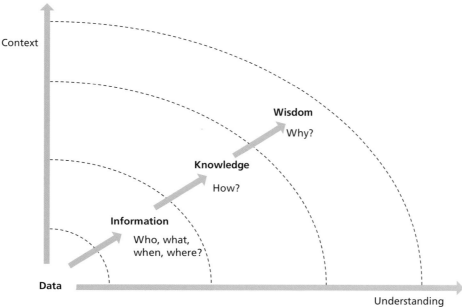

Figure 6.6 The flow from data to wisdom

information (and data). Through the synthesis of these elements, new knowledge is created.

- **Wisdom** makes use of knowledge to create value through correct and well-informed decisions. Wisdom involves having the application and contextual awareness to provide strong common-sense judgement.

The service knowledge management system

> **Definition**
>
> The **service knowledge management system** (SKMS) is a set of tools and databases that is used to manage knowledge, information and data. The service knowledge management system includes tools for collecting, storing, managing, updating, analysing and presenting all the knowledge, information and data that an IT service provider will need to manage the full lifecycle of IT services.

The service knowledge management system includes the configuration management system (CMS), as well as other databases and information systems.

However, clearly the service knowledge management system is a broader concept that covers a much wider base of knowledge, for example:

- The service portfolio
- The definitive media library (DML)
- Service level agreements (SLAs), contracts and operation level agreements (OLAs)
- The information security policy
- The supplier and contract management information system (SCMIS)
- Budgets and cost models
- Business plans
- Continual service improvement (CSI) register and service improvement plans (SIPs)

- Capacity plan and capacity management information system (CMIS)
- Availability plan and availability management system (AMIS)
- Service continuity invocation procedures
- Service reports
- Discussion forum for practitioners
- Project plans
- Known error database (KEDB)
- Skills register
- Diagnostic scripts.

Figure 6.7 illustrates the relationship of the three levels, with configuration data being recorded within the configuration management database (CMDB), and feeding through the configuration management system (CMS) into the service knowledge management system (SKMS) and supporting delivery of the services and informed decision-making.

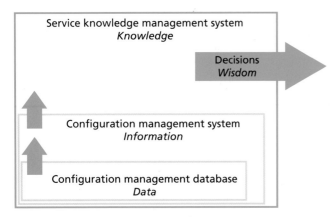

Figure 6.7 Relationship of the CMDB, the CMS and the SKMS

6.6 SAMPLE QUESTIONS

1 Which of the following are the main objectives of the service transition phase of the lifecycle?

1 To ensure the service changes create the expected business value

2 To manage the risks related to the new services as they transition into production

3 To ensure that the services can be used in accordance with the requirements stated within the original service requirements

4 To provide the business with the details of the changing business processes, and carry out subsequent training of these business operational changes

    a 1 and 4 only

    b 2 and 3 only

    c 1, 2 and 3 only

    d All of the above

2 Which of the following are valid items that could be stored in the SKMS?

1 The configuration management system

2 The service portfolio

3 Service level agreements

4 The definitive media library

    a All of the above

    b None of the above

    c 1, and 4 only

    d 1, 3 and 4 only

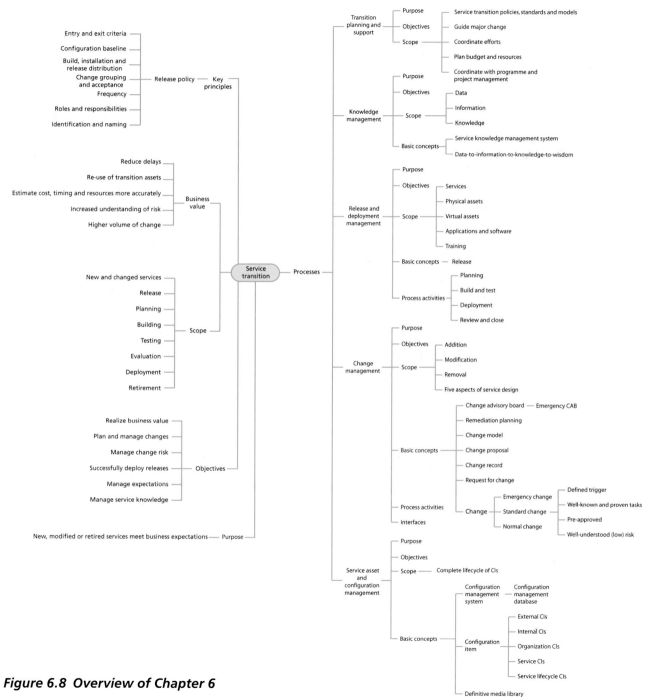

Figure 6.8 Overview of Chapter 6

3   Which of the following is the BEST description of the configuration management system?

    a   A set of tools, data and information that is used to support service asset and configuration management

    b   A component that needs to be managed in order to deliver an IT service

    c   The tools and databases that are used to manage the organization's knowledge and information throughout the whole of the service lifecycle

    d   A single repository holding details of the service model and the relationships between the different components of that service

4   Which of the following describes remediation for a change or release?

    a   Invocation of the ITSC plan

    b   Taking appropriate recovery action following failure of the change or release

    c   Assurance that an emergency change is approved

    d   Predefining steps that should be taken to handle this type of change

5   Which of the following is NOT a valid change type?

    a   Emergency

    b   Standard

    c   Normal

    d   Change proposal

6   Which of the following is the appropriate sequence for the phases of release and deployment?

    a   Plan, do, check, act

    b   Release and deployment planning, release build and test, deployment, review and close

    c   Release build and test, deployment, release and deployment planning, review and close

    d   Review and close, release and deployment planning, release build and test, deployment

Service operation

7

7 Service operation

Strategic objectives are ultimately realized through service operation, requiring effective and efficient delivery and support of services to ensure value for the customer and the service provider.

Case study: service management in practice (Brigitte's experience)

Time has passed and Brigitte is back at the alpine hotel again. Even though she thinks she travels too much, she likes to be back in the beautiful surroundings. She takes a quick walk around the hotel and notices that an expansion with a small water world is almost complete and that the construction of the conference facilities is progressing. She is amazed that the hotel staff are capable of managing two major projects while still running the hotel. After all, it is still the operation of the original part of the hotel that earns the money.

When the new conference services have been implemented, they will have to be operated according to the agreed service levels. Brigitte doesn't know much about hotel operation, but she imagines that it may include activities such as:

- Hosting and facilitation of conferences
- Monitoring and management of the air conditioning in the conference facilities
- Cleaning and maintenance of the conference facilities
- Measurement and reporting of the satisfaction of the conference delegates
- Training of new staff members.

7.1 PURPOSE AND OBJECTIVES

The purpose of the service operation stage is to coordinate and carry out the activities and processes required to deliver and manage services at agreed levels to business users and customers. Service operation is also responsible for the ongoing management of the technology that is used to deliver and support services.

The main objectives of service operation are to:

- Maintain business satisfaction and confidence in IT through effective and efficient delivery and support of agreed IT services
- Minimize the impact of service outages on day-to-day business activities
- Ensure that access to agreed IT services is only provided to those authorized to receive those services.

7.2 SCOPE

Service operation covers:

- All aspects of the end-to-end service agreed with the business, including activities performed by the service provider, external suppliers, the customer or the user of that service
- Service management processes that support the services
- Organizational functions required to deliver and support services

- Technology and infrastructure needed to deliver the services
- People who manage the technology, processes and services.

The following processes are within the scope of service operation:

- Event management
- Incident management
- Request fulfilment
- Problem management
- Access management.

7.3 BUSINESS VALUE

Adopting and implementing consistent approaches for service operation will:

- Reduce unplanned labour and costs for both the business and IT.
- Reduce the duration and frequency of service outages.
- Provide operational results and data that can be used by other ITIL processes to improve services continually.
- Meet the goals and objectives of the organization's security policy by ensuring that IT services will be accessed only by those authorized to use them.
- Provide quick and effective access to standard services which business staff can use to improve their productivity or the quality of business services and products.
- Provide a basis for automated operations.

7.4 KEY PRINCIPLES

7.4.1 Communication

Effective communication in service operation ensures that all teams and departments are able to execute the standard activities involved in delivering services and managing the infrastructure. Issues can often be prevented or mitigated with appropriate communication.

An important principle is that all communication must have an intended purpose or a resultant action. In addition, that the audience should have been actively involved in determining the need for that communication and what they will do with the information.

Types of communication include:

- Routine operational communication
- Communication between shifts
- Performance reporting
- Communication in projects
- Communication related to changes
- Communication related to exceptions and emergencies
- Training of new or customized processes and service designs
- Communication of strategy, design and transition to service operation teams.

There is no definitive medium for communication, nor is there a fixed location or frequency. In some organizations communication has to take place in meetings. Other organizations prefer to use email or the communication inherent in their service management tools.

7.5 PROCESSES

The ITIL Foundation syllabus covers the following service operation processes:

- Event management
- Incident management
- Request fulfilment
- Problem management
- Access management.

7.5.1 Event management

Event management is the process responsible for managing events throughout their lifecycle. Event management is one of the main activities of IT operations.

Case study: service management in practice (Brigitte's experience)

During the next few years Brigitte regularly returns to the hotel. Actually, she went to the grand opening of the new conference centre. The event started in the old reception area where the hotel management proudly presented the control panel for the heating, sun panels and lights in the new conference centre.

Suddenly a beep sounded and a light on the control panel turned red. The face of the man who did the presentation briefly turned pale – he obviously didn't expect an alarm to go off in the middle of his presentation; but, on the other hand, it left him with the opportunity to show how advanced the system was. The beep, he explained, was an announcement from the system that a human intervention was required. In this case the temperature in the auditorium was suddenly unexpectedly low.

To come to this conclusion, the system had collected data from temperature sensors both inside the room and outside the building, as well as data from the heating equipment. The system had then correlated all the information, compared the result with the defined thresholds and issued an alert.

7.5.1.1 Purpose and objectives

The purpose of event management is to manage events throughout their lifecycle. This lifecycle of activities to detect events, make sense of them and determine the appropriate control action is coordinated by the event management process.

The objectives of the event management process are to:

- Detect all changes of state that have significance for the management of a configuration item (CI) or IT service.
- Determine the appropriate control action for events and ensure that these are communicated to the appropriate functions.
- Provide the trigger, or entry point, for the execution of many service operation processes and operations management activities.
- Provide the means to compare actual operating performance and behaviour against design standards and service level agreements (SLAs).
- Provide a basis for service assurance and reporting, and for service improvement.

7.5.1.2 Scope

Event management can be applied to any aspect of service management that needs to be controlled and which can be automated. This includes:

- Configuration items (CIs)
- Environmental conditions (e.g. fire and smoke detection)
- Software licence monitoring for usage to ensure optimum/legal licence utilization and allocation
- Security (e.g. intrusion detection)
- Normal activity (e.g. tracking the use of an application or the performance of a server).

7.5.1.3 Basic concepts

Event

> **Definition**
>
> An **event** is a change of state that has significance for the management of an IT service or other configuration item (CI).

Events are typically notifications created by a service, CI or monitoring tool. Events normally require IT operations personnel to take actions, and often lead to incidents being logged.

Alert

> **Definition**
>
> An **alert** is a notification that a threshold has been reached, something has changed or a failure has occurred.

Alerts are often created and managed by system management tools and are managed by the event management process.

7.5.2 Incident management

Incident management is the process responsible for managing the lifecycle of all incidents.

> **Case study: service management in practice (Brigitte's experience)**
>
> On one of her recent trips, Brigitte one night returned to her room at the hotel to sleep. While brushing her teeth she noticed that the shower head had fallen to the ground and was broken.
>
> After finishing her tooth brushing she dialled the reception. The folder next to the telephone guided her on how to report an incident: 'If you need any kind of assistance or want to report a problem, please call the reception by dialling 1.' The receptionist asked questions such as: 'What is your problem?', 'Is the shower completely useless or can you use it anyway?', 'Is it important to fix it now or can it wait till tomorrow?' and 'When do you plan to take a shower?'
>
> Brigitte didn't need a shower at that moment – but she had to take one in the morning before going back to the factory at 8 a.m. The receptionist was unable to find someone who could fix the shower before 6 a.m. so he tried to identify a workaround: 'Brigitte, do you want to have another room (facing the street so it is a bit noisier) or to have a key to the pool area and have your morning shower there?'

7.5.2.1 Purpose and objectives

The purpose of incident management is to restore normal service operation as quickly as possible and minimize the adverse impact on business operations, thus ensuring that agreed levels of service quality are maintained. 'Normal service operation' is defined as an operational state where services and configuration items (CIs) are performing within their agreed service and operational levels.

The objectives of the incident management process are to:

- Ensure that standardized methods and procedures are used for efficient and prompt response, analysis, documentation, ongoing management and reporting of incidents
- Increase visibility and communication of incidents to business and IT support staff
- Align incident management activities and priorities with those of the business
- Maintain user satisfaction with the quality of IT services.

7.5.2.2 Scope

Incident management includes any event which disrupts, or which could disrupt, a service. This includes events which are communicated directly by users, either through the service desk or through an interface from event management to incident management tools.

Incidents can also be reported and/or logged by technical staff. This does not mean, however, that all events are incidents. Many classes of events are not related to disruptions at all, but are indicators of normal operation or are simply informational.

Although both incidents and service requests are reported to the service desk, this does not mean that they are the same. Service requests do not represent a disruption to agreed service, but are a way of meeting the customer's needs and may be addressing an agreed target in a service level agreement (SLA). Service requests are dealt with by the request fulfilment process.

7.5.2.3 Basic concepts

Incident and workaround

> **Definition**
>
> An **incident** is an unplanned interruption to an IT service or reduction in the quality of an IT service. Failure of a configuration item that has not yet affected service is also an incident – for example, failure of one disk from a mirror set.

In some cases it may be possible to find a workaround to an incident – a temporary way of overcoming the difficulties. But it is important that work on a permanent resolution continues where this is justified.

> **Definition**
>
> A **workaround** is a way of reducing or eliminating the impact of an incident or problem for which a full resolution is not yet available.

Examples would be restarting a failed configuration item (CI) or by making a manual amendment to an input file to allow a program to complete its run successfully.

Workarounds for problems (see section 7.5.4) are documented in known error records. Workarounds for incidents that do not have associated problem records are documented in the incident record.

Prioritization

An important aspect of logging every incident is to agree and allocate an appropriate priority – as this will determine how the incident is handled both by support tools and support staff.

An effective way of calculating these elements and deriving an overall priority level for each incident is shown in Figure 7.1.

An indication of impact is often the number of users being affected. However, in some cases the loss of service to a single user can have a major business impact, so numbers alone are not enough to evaluate overall priority. Other factors that can also contribute to impact levels are:

- Risk to life or limb
- The number of services affected – may be multiple services
- The level of financial losses
- Effect on business reputation
- Regulatory or legislative breaches.

Timescales must be agreed for all incident-handling stages, depending on the priority of the incident – based on the overall incident response and resolution targets within service level agreements (SLAs) – and captured as targets within operational level

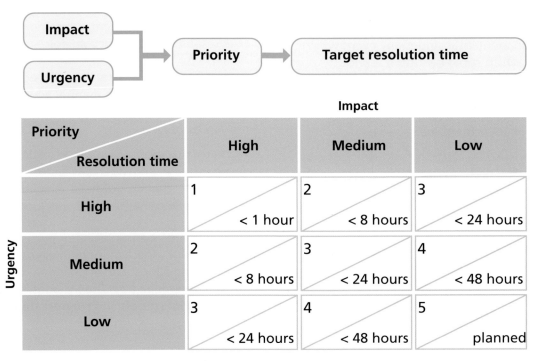

Figure 7.1 Example of calculation of priority based on impact and urgency

agreements (OLAs) and underpinning contracts. All support groups should be made fully aware of these timescales.

Major incident

A separate procedure, with shorter timescales and greater urgency, must be used for major incidents. A definition of what constitutes a major incident must be agreed and ideally mapped onto the overall incident prioritization system – such that it will be dealt with through this separate procedure.

Where necessary, the major incident procedure should include the establishment of a separate major incident team under the direct leadership of the incident manager, formulated to concentrate on this incident alone to ensure that adequate resources and focus are provided to finding a swift resolution.

Incident model

Many incidents are not new. They involve dealing with something that has happened before and may well happen again. For this reason, some organizations find it helpful to predefine incident models.

Definition

An **incident model** is a way of predefining the steps that should be taken to handle a process for dealing with a particular type of incident in an agreed way.

The incident model should include:

- The steps that should be taken to handle the incident
- The chronological order these steps should be taken in, with any dependences or co-processing defined
- Responsibilities: who should do what

- Precautions to be taken before resolving the incident, such as backing up data and configuration files, or taking steps to comply with health- and safety-related guidelines
- Timescales and thresholds for completion of the actions
- Escalation procedures: who should be contacted and when
- Any necessary evidence-preservation activities.

7.5.2.4 Process activities

The key activities within the incident management process include (as shown in Figure 7.2):

- **Incident identification** Incidents may be detected by event management, by calls to the service desk, from web or other self-help interfaces, or directly by technical staff. Service requests or change requests incorrectly logged as incidents are identified so that they can be passed to the request fulfilment or change management processes respectively.
- **Incident logging** All incidents must be logged and time-stamped, regardless of whether they are received through a service desk telephone call or whether automatically detected via an event alert. The log must include sufficient data to enable the incident to be managed.
- **Incident categorization** Categories are used to identify the type of incident and assist with trending analysis. Multi-level categorization can be used to identify multiple levels of categories that can be associated with an incident, as shown in Figure 7.3.

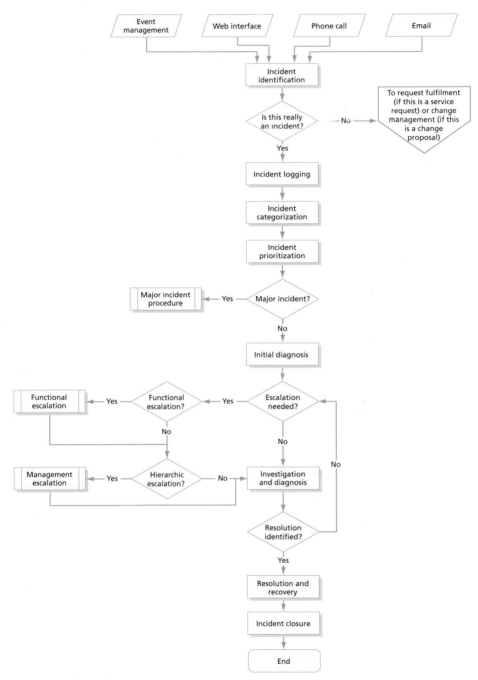

Figure 7.2 Incident management process flow

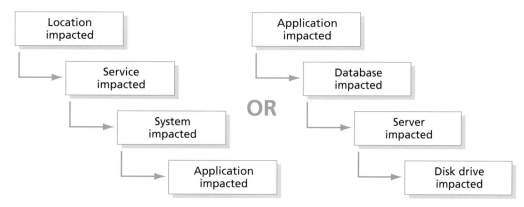

Figure 7.3 Multi-level incident categorization

- **Incident prioritization** A priority is assigned based on impact and urgency. Priorities are dynamic and may be changed during the life of the incident.
- **Initial diagnosis** If possible, the incident should be resolved while the user is still on the phone. Sometimes the service desk analyst will continue work on the incident and contact the user when it has been resolved. An incident-matching procedure can be developed to help service desk and other support staff match incidents with known errors, problems or other incidents to find resolutions quickly where possible.
- **Incident escalation**
  - **Functional escalation** The incident is transferred to a technical team with a higher level of expertise.
  - **Hierarchic escalation** If incidents are of a serious nature, the appropriate managers must be notified – for informational purposes at least.
- **Investigation and diagnosis** Each of the support groups involved with the incident handling will investigate and diagnose what has gone wrong.

- **Resolution and recovery** When a potential resolution has been identified, this should be tested, applied and documented.
- **Incident closure** The service desk should check that the incident is fully resolved and that the users are satisfied and willing to agree that the incident can be closed.

7.5.2.5 Interfaces

The interfaces with incident management include:

- **Service level management** The ability to resolve incidents in a specified time is a key part of delivering an agreed level of service.
- **Availability management** Availability management will use incident management data to determine the availability of IT services and look at where the incident lifecycle can be improved.
- **Capacity management** Incident management provides a trigger for performance monitoring where there appears to be a performance problem.
- **Information security management** Incident management provides security-related incident information for security management.

- **Service asset and configuration management** This provides the data used to identify and progress incidents.
- **Change management** Where a change is required to implement a workaround or resolution, this will need to be logged as an RFC and progressed through change management.
- **Problem management** Incident management forms part of the overall process of dealing with problems in the organization. Incidents are often caused by underlying problems, which must be solved to prevent the incident from recurring. Incident management provides a point where these are reported.

7.5.3 Request fulfilment

Request fulfilment is the process responsible for managing the lifecycle of all service requests.

> **Case study: service management in practice (Brigitte's experience)**
>
> On another trip, Brigitte had forgotten her alarm clock so she needed to find another way to get a wake-up call. The hotel room contained an interactive television with a multitude of service menus. She turned on the television and went to the self-service menu (1. Wake-up service, 2. Restaurant menu, 3. Reservation of restaurant tables, 4. Room service, 5. Opening hours in pool area etc.). She pressed '1' and '0630' to set the alarm for 6.30 a.m.
>
> Brigitte reflected on the service system. It was quite smart – the guests were able to see most of the services provided and the system even handled a lot of them without human intervention.

7.5.3.1 Purpose and objectives

The purpose of request fulfilment is to manage the lifecycle of all service requests from the users.

The objectives of the request fulfilment process are to:

- Maintain user and customer satisfaction through efficient and professional handling of all service requests
- Provide a channel for users to request and receive standard services for which a predefined authorization and qualification process exists
- Provide information to users and customers about the availability of services and the procedure for obtaining them
- Source and deliver the components of requested standard services (e.g. licences and software media)
- Assist with general information, complaints or comments.

7.5.3.2 Scope

The process needed to fulfil a request will vary depending upon exactly what is being requested but can usually be broken down into a set of activities that have to be performed. For each request, these activities should be documented into a request model.

Ultimately it is up to each organization to decide and document which service requests it will handle through the request fulfilment process and which will have to go through other processes such as business relationship management for dealing with requests for new or changed services.

7.5.3.3 Basic concepts

Service request

> **Definition**
>
> A **service request** is a formal request from a user for something to be provided – for example, a request for information, or advice; to reset a password; or to install a workstation for a new user. Service requests may be linked to a request for change as part of fulfilling the request.

Service requests are managed by the request fulfilment process, usually in conjunction with the service desk. The term 'service request' is used as a generic description for the many different types of demand that are placed on the IT organization by users. Many of these are typically requests for small changes that are low risk, frequently performed, low cost etc. (e.g. a request to change a password, a request to install an additional software application onto a particular workstation, a request to relocate some items of desktop equipment) or may be just a request for information.

7.5.4 Problem management

Problem management is the process responsible for managing the lifecycle of the underlying causes of one or more incidents.

> **Case study: service management in practice (Brigitte's experience)**
>
> One time when Brigitte visited the hotel, the shower head had been broken; as a result she had had to go to the pool area to have her morning shower. Because of this, the first thing Brigitte did when she arrived at the hotel room next time was to check if the shower was OK. Not only was it OK but also a strap had been mounted on the shower head to prevent it from falling to the floor if dropped.

Brigitte had not been the only one with a shower head problem; a number of incidents had been reported, and an analysis was performed to identify the root causes of the problem. It turned out that the root causes were weaknesses in the shower heads combined with human behaviour. A number of solutions were examined before the problem was fixed, including replacement of all shower heads and mounting of a strap that prevents the shower heads from falling.

7.5.4.1 Purpose and objectives

The purpose of problem management is to manage the lifecycle of all problems, from first identification through further investigation and documentation to eventual removal. Problem management seeks to minimize the adverse impact of incidents and problems on the business that are caused by underlying errors within the IT infrastructure, and to proactively prevent any recurrence of incidents related to these errors. In order to achieve this, problem management seeks to get to the root cause of incidents, document and communicate known errors, and initiate actions to improve or correct the situation.

The objectives of the problem management process are to:

- Prevent problems and resulting incidents from happening
- Eliminate recurring incidents
- Minimize the impact of incidents that cannot be prevented.

7.5.4.2 Scope

Problem management includes the activities required to diagnose the root cause of incidents and to determine the resolution of those problems. It is also responsible for ensuring that the resolution is implemented through the appropriate control procedures, especially change management and release and deployment management.

Problem management will maintain information about problems and the appropriate workarounds and resolutions, so that the organization is able to reduce the number and impact of incidents over time.

Although incident and problem management are separate processes, they are closely related, will typically use the same tools and may use similar categorization, impact and priority coding systems. This will ensure effective communication when dealing with related incidents and problems.

The problem management process has both reactive and proactive aspects.

7.5.4.3 Basic concepts

Incidents versus problems

An incident is an unplanned interruption to an IT service or reduction in the quality of an IT service. A problem presents a different view of an incident by understanding its underlying cause, which may also be the cause of other incidents. Incidents do not 'become' problems. While incident management activities are focused on restoring services to normal-state operations, problem management activities are focused on finding ways to prevent incidents from happening in the first place.

Problem, known error and resolution

> **Definition**
>
> A **problem** is a cause of one or more incidents.

The cause is not usually known at the time when a problem record is created, and the problem management process is responsible for further investigation.

> **Definition**
>
> A **known error** is a problem that has a documented root cause and a workaround.

Known errors are created and managed throughout their lifecycle by problem management. Known errors may also be identified by development staff or suppliers.

As soon as the diagnosis is complete, and particularly where a workaround has been found, a known error record must be raised and placed in the known error database (KEDB) so that if further incidents or problems arise they can be identified and the service restored more quickly.

However, in some cases it may be advantageous to raise a known error record even earlier in the overall process, for example just for information purposes, even though the diagnosis may not be complete or a workaround found. So it is inadvisable to set a concrete procedural point specifying exactly when a known error record must be raised. It should be done as soon as it becomes useful to do so.

> **Definition**
>
> A **resolution** is an action taken to repair the root cause of an incident or problem, or to implement a workaround.

Once a root cause has been found and a solution to remove it has been developed, this should be applied to resolve the problem. In reality, safeguards may be needed to ensure that the resolution does not cause further difficulties.

If a workaround is found, it is important that the problem record remains open and details of the workaround are documented within the problem record.

If any change to a configuration item (CI) is required, this will require a request for change (RFC) to be raised and authorized before the resolution can be applied.

Known error database

To allow quicker diagnosis and resolution of incidents and problems, previous knowledge of how they were overcome should be stored in a known error database (KEDB).

The KEDB should be used during the incident and problem diagnosis phases to try to speed up the resolution process – and new records should be added as quickly as possible when a new problem has been identified and diagnosed.

The known error record should hold exact details of the fault and the symptoms that occurred, together with precise details of any workaround or resolution action that can be taken to restore the service and resolve the problem.

The KEDB, like the configuration management system (CMS), forms part of the larger service knowledge management system (SKMS).

Problem model

Many problems will be unique and will require handling in an individual way. However, it is conceivable that some incidents may recur because of dormant or underlying problems.

As well as creating a known error record in the known error database (KEDB) to ensure quicker diagnosis, the creation of a model for handling such problems in the future may be helpful.

7.5.4.4 Process activities

Problem management consists of two major processes:

- **Reactive problem management** is concerned with solving problems in response to one or more incidents. Reactive problem management complements incident management activities by focusing on the underlying cause of an incident to prevent its recurrence and identifying workarounds when necessary.
- **Proactive problem management** is concerned with identifying and solving problems and known errors before further related incidents can occur again. With proactive problem management, process activities are triggered by activities seeking to improve services. In that way proactive problem management complements continual service improvement (CSI) activities by helping to identify workarounds and actions that can improve the quality of a service.

The problem management process is shown in Figure 7.4. This is a simplified chart to show the normal process flow, but in reality some of the states may be iterative or variations may have to be made in order to handle particular situations.

The key activities within the problem management process include:

- **Problem detection** There are multiple ways of detecting problems. These can include triggers for reactive and proactive problem management.

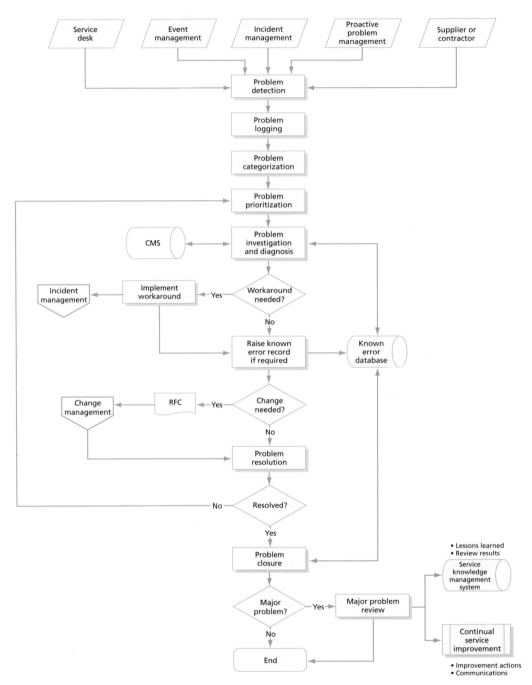

Figure 7.4 Problem management process flow

Reactive problem management triggers are:

- When an incident is reported to the service desk and the cause of it is unknown, even if the incident itself may be resolved by applying a workaround
- When a technical support group or a supplier or contractor identifies that a problem exists
- When monitoring tools detect an infrastructure failure, which could lead to both an incident and a problem being identified
- When a problem is discovered as a result of proactive problem management.

Proactive problem management triggers are:

- Analysis of incidents
- Trending of historical incident records
- Service improvement activities.

■ **Problem logging** All problems must be logged, and problem records must include all the details needed to manage the problem through its lifecycle, including links to related incidents.

■ **Problem categorization** Problems are categorized to enable analysis and reporting. It is advisable to use the same coding system as for incidents.

■ **Problem prioritization** Problems should be prioritized in the same way and for the same reason as incidents. Problem priority should take into account the frequency and impact of related incidents. Problem priority is also based on the severity of the problem, which is a measure of how serious the problem is from an infrastructure perspective – e.g. how long it will take to fix or how much it will cost.

■ **Problem investigation and diagnosis** An investigation diagnoses the root cause of the problem. The speed and nature of the investigation, and the resources invested, should depend on impact, severity and urgency of the problem.

■ **Workarounds** A workaround is a way of reducing or eliminating the impact of a problem, but not fully resolving its cause. If a workaround has been implemented, the problem record should remain open until the problem has been resolved.

■ **Raising a known error record** When diagnosis is complete, and particularly when a workaround has been found, a known error record should be raised and stored in the known error database (KEDB) so that further incidents or problems can be identified and the service restored more quickly. Sometimes it may be advantageous to raise a known error record earlier in the overall process.

■ **Problem resolution** Once a root cause has been found and a solution to remove it has been developed, the solution should be applied to resolve the problem. Full resolution of a problem usually involves raising a change request. If the problem is very serious, this may be an emergency change request. Sometimes it may not be possible to justify the change in a business case, and a decision may be made to leave the problem record open and rely on the workaround in the known error record.

■ **Problem closure** When a final solution has been applied, the problem record and related incident records should be closed. The record should be checked to ensure that it contains all required information, and the status of related known error records should be updated.

■ **Major problem review** A review of every major problem should be conducted to learn lessons for the future. 'Major problem' is defined by the priority system.

7.5.4.5 Interfaces

The interfaces with problem management include:

- **Service level management** The occurrence of incidents and problems affects the level of service delivery measured by service level management.
- **Availability management** This is involved with determining how to reduce downtime and increase uptime.
- **Capacity management** Some problems will require investigation by capacity management teams and techniques, e.g. performance issues.
- **IT service continuity management** Problem management acts as an entry point into IT service continuity management where a significant problem is not resolved before it starts to have a major impact on the business.
- **Service asset and configuration management** Problem management uses the configuration management system (CMS) to identify faulty configuration items (CIs) and also to determine the impact of problems and resolutions.
- **Change management** Problem management ensures that all resolutions or workarounds that require a change to a CI are submitted through change management.
- **Release and deployment management** This is responsible for rolling out problem fixes into the live environment.
- **Knowledge management** The service knowledge management system (SKMS) can be used to form the basis of the known error database (KEDB) and hold (or integrate with) the problem records.
- **Incident management** Incident management forms part of the overall process of dealing with problems in the organization. Incidents are often caused by underlying problems, which must be solved to prevent the incident from recurring. Incident management provides a point where these are reported.
- **The seven-step improvement process** The occurrence of incidents and problems provides a basis for identifying opportunities for service improvement and adding them to the continual service improvement (CSI) register.

7.5.5 Access management

Access management is the process responsible for allowing users to make use of IT services, data or other assets. Access management helps to protect the confidentiality, integrity and availability of assets by ensuring that only authorized users are able to access or modify the assets. Access management implements the policies of information security management and is sometimes referred to as rights management or identity management.

7.5.5.1 Purpose and objectives

The purpose of access management is to provide the right for users to be able to use a service or group of services, i.e. the execution of policies and actions defined in information security management.

The objectives of the access management process are to:

- Manage access to services based on policies and actions defined in information security management
- Efficiently respond to requests for granting access to services, changing access rights or restricting access, ensuring that the rights being provided or changed are properly granted
- Oversee access to services and ensure that rights provided are not improperly used.

Brigitte recalls the stay when the shower head was broken. She was not able to use the shower in her room and had to shower in the pool area. But the pool area was usually closed at the time when Brigitte needed to shower.

Therefore the receptionist helped her with getting access to the area:

- She checked the (security) policy to see if she was allowed to give a guest access to the pool area outside normal openings hours.
- Then she identified Brigitte's card key in the hotel's database.
- With that information she used the card key system to grant Brigitte the rights to enter the pool area outside normal opening hours.
- And finally she filed a note about what she had done to ensure that Brigitte's card key rights would be returned to normal when the shower head was fixed.

7.5.5.2 Scope

Access management is effectively the execution of the policies in information security management, in that it enables the organization to manage the confidentiality, availability and integrity of the organization's data and intellectual property.

Access management ensures that users are given the right to use a service, but it does not ensure that this access is available at all agreed times – this is provided by availability management.

Access management can be initiated by a service request.

7.5.5.3 Basic concepts

Access, identity and rights

Access management is the process that enables users to use the services that are documented in the service catalogue. It comprises the following basic concepts of access, identity and rights.

Definitions

Access refers to the level and extent of a service's functionality or data that a user is entitled to use.

Identity refers to a unique name that is used to identify a user, person or role. The identity is used to grant rights to that user, person or role.

Examples of identities might be the username SmithJ or the role 'change manager'.

Definition

Rights (also called privileges) are the entitlements, or permissions, granted to a user or role – for example, the right to modify particular data, or to authorize a change.

Typical rights, or levels of access, are: read, write, execute, change and delete.

7.6 FUNCTIONS

7.6.1 Service desk

7.6.1.1 Role

A service desk is a functional unit made up of a dedicated number of staff responsible for dealing with a variety of service activities, usually made via telephone calls or web interface, or automatically reported infrastructure events.

The service desk is a vitally important part of an IT organization and should be the single point of contact for IT users on a day-by-day basis. It not only handles incidents, escalates incidents to problem management staff, manages service requests and answers questions; it may also provide an interface for other activities such as customer change requests, maintenance contracts, software licences, service level management, service asset and configuration management, availability management, financial management for IT services, and IT service continuity management.

A good service desk can compensate for deficiencies elsewhere in the IT organization, but a poor service desk can give a poor impression of an otherwise very effective IT organization.

The exact nature, size, type and location of a service desk will vary, depending upon the type of business, number of users, geography, complexity of calls, scope of services, and many other factors.

7.6.1.2   Objectives

The primary objective of the service desk is to provide a single point of contact (SPOC) between the services being provided and the users. Service desk staff execute the incident management and request fulfilment processes to restore the normal-state service operation to the users as quickly as possible. In this context 'restoration of service' is meant in the widest possible sense. While this could be fixing a technical fault, it could equally involve fulfilling a service request or answering a query – anything that is needed to allow users to return to working satisfactorily.

Specific responsibilities of the service desk are:

- Logging all relevant incident and service request details, and allocating categorization and prioritization codes
- Providing first-line investigation and diagnosis
- Resolving incidents and service requests when first contacted whenever possible
- Escalating incidents and service requests that they cannot resolve within agreed timescales
- Keeping users informed of progress
- Closing all resolved incidents, requests and other calls
- Conducting customer/user satisfaction call-backs/surveys
- Communication with users
- Updating the configuration management system (CMS) if so agreed.

7.6.1.3   Organizational structures

There are many ways of structuring service desks and locating them. The main options are:

- Local service desk
- Centralized service desk
- Virtual service desk
- Follow-the-sun.

In reality, an organization may have to implement a structure that combines a number of these options in order to fully meet the business needs.

Local service desk

This is where a service desk is co-located within or physically close to the user community it serves (see Figure 7.5).

A local service desk often aids communication and gives a clearly visible presence, and can support local language, cultural differences, different time zones or specialized groups or users. However, it can often be inefficient and expensive to resource, as local staff are tied up waiting to deal with incidents and service requests when the volume and arrival rate of calls may not justify this.

Centralized service desk

It is possible to reduce the number of service desks by merging them into a single location or a smaller number of locations by drawing the staff into one or more centralized service desk structures (Figure 7.6).

Centralized service desks can be more efficient and cost-effective, allowing fewer overall staff to deal with a higher volume of calls. It might still be necessary to maintain some form of local presence to handle physical support requirements, but such staff can be controlled and deployed from the central desk.

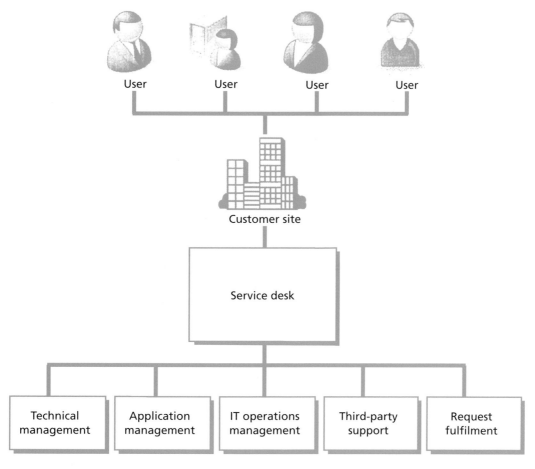

Figure 7.5 Local service desk

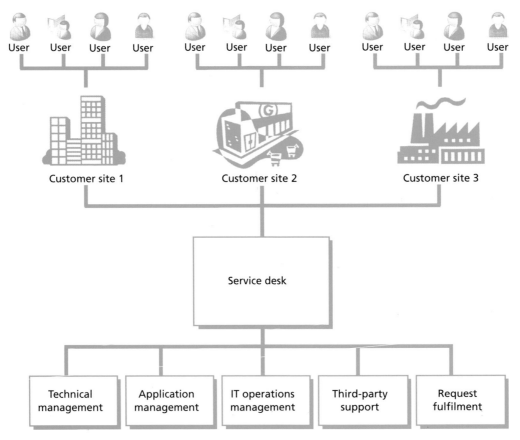

Figure 7.6 Centralized service desk

Virtual service desk

Through the use of technology, particularly the internet, and the use of corporate support tools, it is possible to give the impression of a single, centralized service desk when in fact the personnel may be spread or located in any number or types of geographical or structural locations (see Figure 7.7).

Virtual service desks bring in the option of home working, secondary support groups, off-shoring or outsourcing, or any combination necessary to meet user demand.

Follow-the-sun

Some global or international organizations may wish to combine two or more of their geographically dispersed service desks to provide a 24-hour follow-the-sun service. For example, a service desk in the Asia-Pacific region may deal with calls during its standard office hours, and at the end of this period it may hand over responsibility for any open incidents to a European-based desk. This kind of arrangement can give 24-hour coverage at relatively low cost, as no desk has to work more than a single shift. However,

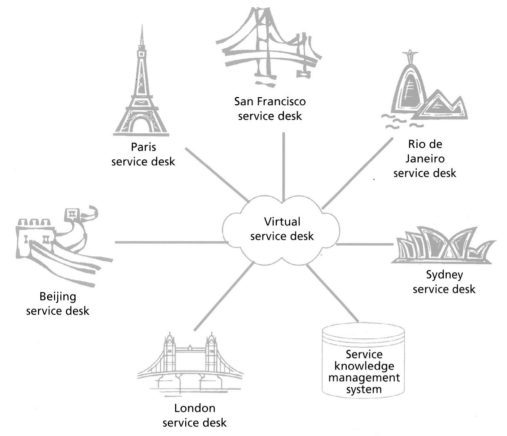

Figure 7.7 Virtual service desk

common processes, tools, shared databases of information and culture must be addressed for this approach to succeed – and well-controlled escalation and handover procedures are needed.

7.6.2 Technical management

7.6.2.1 Role

Technical management refers to the groups, departments or teams that provide technical expertise and management of the IT infrastructure. Technical management plays a dual role:

■ It is the custodian of technical knowledge and expertise related to managing the IT infrastructure. In this role technical management ensures that the knowledge required to design, test, manage and improve IT services is identified, developed and refined.

■ It provides the actual resources to support the service lifecycle. In this role technical management ensures that resources are effectively trained and deployed to design, build, transition, operate and improve the technology required to deliver and support IT services.

An additional, but very important role played by technical management is to provide guidance to IT operations about how best to carry out the ongoing operational management of technology.

7.6.2.2 Objectives

The objectives of technical management are to help plan, implement and maintain a stable technical infrastructure to support the organization's business processes through:

■ Well-designed and highly resilient, cost-effective technical topology

■ The use of adequate technical skills to maintain the technical infrastructure in optimum condition

■ Swift use of technical skills to speedily diagnose and resolve any technical failures that occur.

7.6.3 IT operations management

7.6.3.1 Role

IT operations management is responsible for performing the day-to-day operational activities required to manage and maintain the IT infrastructure and deliver the agreed level of IT services to the business.

The role of IT operations management is to execute the ongoing activities and procedures required to manage and maintain the IT infrastructure. These activities include:

■ **IT operations control** Oversees the execution and monitoring of the operational activities and events in the IT infrastructure. In addition, IT operations control also performs the following specific tasks:
  ● Console management
  ● Job scheduling
  ● Backup and restore
  ● Print and output management
  ● Maintenance activities.

■ **Facilities management** Manages the physical IT environment – typically a data centre or computer rooms and recovery sites together with power and cooling equipment.

As with many IT service management processes and functions, IT operations management plays a dual role:

■ It is responsible for executing the activities and performance standards defined during service design and tested during service transition.

■ In addition IT operations is part of the process of adding value to the different lines of business and supporting the value network.

7.6.3.2 Objectives

The objectives of IT operations management include:

■ Achieving the stability of an organization's day-to-day processes and activities

■ Implementing regular improvements to achieve better service at reduced costs, while maintaining stability

■ Swift application of operational skills to diagnose and resolve any IT operations failures that occur.

7.6.4 Application management

7.6.4.1 Role

Application management is responsible for managing applications throughout their lifecycle. This differs from application development, as application management covers the entire ongoing lifecycle of an application, including requirements, design, build, deploy, operate and

Table 7.1 Application development versus application management

	Application development	Application management
Nature of activities	One-time set of activities to design and construct application solutions	Ongoing set of activities to oversee and manage applications throughout their entire lifecycle
Scope of activities	Performed mostly for applications developed in house	Performed for all applications, whether purchased from third parties or developed in house
Primary focus	Utility focus Building functionality for the customer What the application does is more important than how it is operated	Both utility and warranty focus What the functionality is as well as how to deliver it Manageability aspects of the application, i.e. how to ensure stability and performance of the application
Management mode	Most development work is done in projects where the focus is on delivering specific units of work to specification, on time and within budget This means that it is often difficult for developers to understand and build for ongoing operations, especially because they are not available for support of the application once they have moved on to the next project	Most work is done as part of repeatable, ongoing processes. A relatively small number of people work in projects This means that it is very difficult for operational staff to get involved in development projects, as that takes them away from their ongoing operational responsibilities
Measurement	Staff are typically rewarded for creativity and for completing one project so that they can move on to the next project	Staff are typically rewarded for consistency and for preventing unexpected events and unauthorized functionality (e.g. 'bells and whistles' added by developers)
Cost	Development projects are relatively easy to quantify because the resources are known and it is easy to link their expenses to a specific application or IT service	Ongoing management costs are often mixed in with the costs of other IT services because resources are often shared across multiple IT services and applications
Lifecycles	Development staff focus on software development lifecycles, which highlight the dependencies for successful operation, but do not assign accountability for these	Staff involved in ongoing management typically only control one or two stages of these lifecycles – operation and improvement

optimize. Application development is mainly concerned with the one-time activities for requirements, design and build of applications.

Application management may be involved in development projects, but application management staff are not usually the same as the application development teams. Each team manages its own environment in its own way and each has a separate interface to the business. This is illustrated in Table 7.1.

Application management has several roles:

- It is the custodian of technical knowledge and expertise related to managing applications. In this role application management, working together with technical management, ensures that the knowledge required to design, test, manage and improve IT services is identified, developed and refined.
- It provides the actual resources to support the service lifecycle. In this role application management ensures that resources are effectively trained and deployed to design, build, transition, operate and improve the technology required to deliver and support IT services.

- It provides guidance to IT operations about how best to carry out the ongoing operational management of applications.
- It integrates the application management lifecycle into the service lifecycle.

7.6.4.2 Objectives

The objectives of application management are to support the organization's business processes by helping to identify functional and manageability requirements for application software, and then to assist in the design and deployment of those applications and to provide ongoing support and improvement of those applications.

These objectives are achieved through:

- Applications that are well-designed, resilient and cost-effective
- Ensuring that the required functionality is available to achieve the required business outcome
- Ensuring the organization of adequate technical skills to maintain operational applications in optimum condition
- Swift use of technical skills to speedily diagnose and resolve any technical failures that occur.

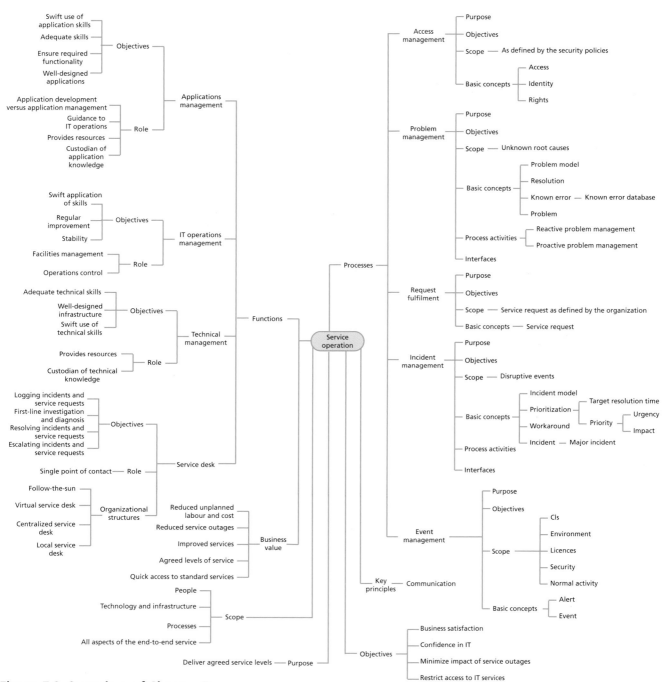

Figure 7.8 Overview of Chapter 7

7.7 SAMPLE QUESTIONS

1 Which of the following is the PRIMARY objective of service operation?

a To ensure that the services are designed to meet the stated business objectives and that the four Ps have been considered

b To ensure that the service can be used in accordance with the requirements and constraints specified within the service requirements

c To carry out activities and processes required to deliver and manage services at agreed levels

d To manage the technology that is used to deliver and support the services

2 Which roles within the organization will take responsibility for carrying out the activities within the incident management process?

1 The incident management process owner

2 The service desk

3 Technical management

4 Application management

   a 1 only

   b 2 only

   c 2, 3 and 4 only

   d 1 and 2 only

3 Which of the following is the PRIMARY purpose of problem management?

a To understand the root cause of one or more incidents and identify a fix

b To manage major incidents

c To restore service as quickly as possible and minimize the adverse impact on business operations

d To provide a workaround on all problems

4 In which of the following circumstances should an incident be generated following an event notification?

a An incident should always be raised following an event

b An incident should never be raised following an event

c An incident should be raised following an alert

d An incident should be raised when there has been a disruption to service

5 Which of the following is NOT a valid type of service desk described within ITIL service operation?

a Local service desk

b Centralized service desk

c Technical service desk

d Virtual service desk

6 When an incident is logged the service desk should give it a priority rating. What is this based on?

a The speed with which it can be resolved

b Its impact on business operation and its urgency

c The customer's perception of priority

d Whether there is a problem record related to it

Continual service improvement

8

8 Continual service improvement

Continual service improvement is responsible for managing improvements to services and service assets to align these with changing business needs. The performance of the service provider is continually measured, and improvements are made to services, capabilities and resources in order to increase efficiency, effectiveness and cost effectiveness.

Case study: service management in practice (Brigitte's experience)

On the desk in Brigitte's room the hotel staff always leave a guest satisfaction form. The form contains statements like 'The room is clean' and she is asked to state to what degree she agrees.

Brigitte is an auditor in the pharmaceutical industry, so for professional reasons she is rather curious to get insight into the quality management practices of the hotel. Brigitte asks the receptionist at the front desk. Fortunately, as there are no other guests in the reception area there is time for a deeper conversation and the following points emerge:

■ The hotel is working with formally defined processes and procedures. The processes ensure that the hotel meets (or exceeds) the quality expectations of the guests in an efficient manner.

■ To ensure that processes continually reflect the changing requirements of the guests and the hotel infrastructure, a quality management system has been established. This quality management system also aims at improving the effectiveness and efficiency of the processes.

■ The form that Brigitte has just filled in is part of that quality system. The purpose is to measure and, if needed, adjust the effectiveness of the processes. For example, the cleaning procedures have just been improved because of general dissatisfaction with the cleaning standard. The forms have been handed out to the guests before and after the change, to measure and control that the cleaning quality has improved satisfactorily.

■ After the forms have been collected they are analysed. The results are presented to the management, who decide whether anything has to be changed. The result is presented to the hotel cleaners; it is hoped that the opinion of the guests will convince them that the change in the way they are working was a good idea (there was some resistance when the new process was introduced).

The receptionist continues to explain that before the hotel launched its conference services she attended a meeting where staff discussed whether the quality management system was to be improved to support the new conference services. Among other issues, they evaluated whether the system would be able to identify the needs for improvement activities such as:

- Enhancing the booking process
- Developing the training programme for new staff members
- Renovating conference facilities after a couple of years.

Because it turned out that the system at the time wasn't able to capture important future quality issues, the staff agreed to improve the quality management system before launching the conference services.

8.1 PURPOSE AND OBJECTIVES

The purpose of the continual service improvement (CSI) stage is to align IT services with changing business needs by identifying and implementing improvements to IT services that support business processes. These improvement activities support the lifecycle approach through service strategy, service design, service transition and service operation. Continual service improvement is always seeking ways to improve service effectiveness, process effectiveness and cost effectiveness.

The main objectives of continual service improvement are to:

- Review, analyse and make recommendations on improvement opportunities in each lifecycle stage
- Review and analyse service-level achievement results

- Identify and implement activities to improve IT service quality and improve the efficiency and effectiveness of the enabling processes
- Improve the cost effectiveness of delivering IT services without sacrificing customer satisfaction
- Ensure that applicable quality management methods are used to support continual improvement activities
- Understand what to measure, why it is being measured and what the successful outcome should be.

8.2 SCOPE

Continual service improvement covers:

- The overall health of IT service management as a discipline
- The continual alignment of the service portfolio with current and future business needs
- The maturity and capability of the organization, management, processes and people utilized by the services
- Continual improvement of all aspects of the IT services and the service assets that support them.

Only one process is within the scope of continual service improvement: the seven-step improvement process.

8.3 BUSINESS VALUE

Adopting and implementing consistent approaches for continual service improvement will:

- Lead to a gradual and continual improvement in service quality, where justified
- Ensure that IT services remain continuously aligned to business requirements

■ Result in gradual improvements in cost effectiveness through a reduction in costs and/or the capability to handle more work at the same cost

■ Use monitoring and reporting to identify opportunities for improvement in all lifecycle stages and in all processes.

8.4 KEY PRINCIPLES

8.4.1 Deming Cycle

W. Edwards Deming is best known for proposing the Deming Cycle for quality improvement. The four key stages of the cycle are Plan, Do, Check, Act (PDCA) as illustrated in Figure 8.1. Our goal in using the Deming Cycle is steady, ongoing improvement. It is a fundamental tenet of continual service improvement (CSI).

8.4.1.1 Plan

Establish goals for improvement (including gap analysis), define action steps to close the gap, and establish and implement measures to ensure that the gap has been closed and benefits achieved.

8.4.1.2 Do

Develop and implement a project or initiative to close the gap (e.g. implementation or improvement of processes and establishing the smooth operation of the process).

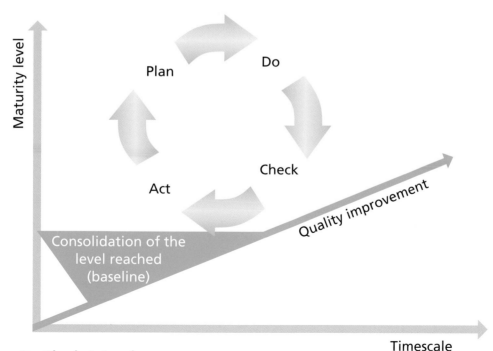

Figure 8.1 Plan-Do-Check-Act cycle

8.4.1.3 Check

Compare the implemented environment with the measures of success established in the plan phase. The comparison determines if a gap still exists between the improvement objectives of the process and the operational process state. Gaps don't necessarily require closure. A gap may be considered tolerable if the actual performance is within allowable limits of performance.

8.4.1.4 Act

Determine whether further work is required to close remaining gaps, and allocate resources necessary to support another round of improvement. Project decisions at this stage are the input for the next round of the lifecycle, closing the loop as input to the plan phase.

8.4.2 The continual service improvement approach

Figure 8.2 shows an overall approach to CSI and illustrates a continual cycle of improvement based on the Deming Cycle.

This approach to improvement can be summarized as follows:

■ Embrace the vision by understanding the high-level business objectives. The vision should align the business and IT strategies.

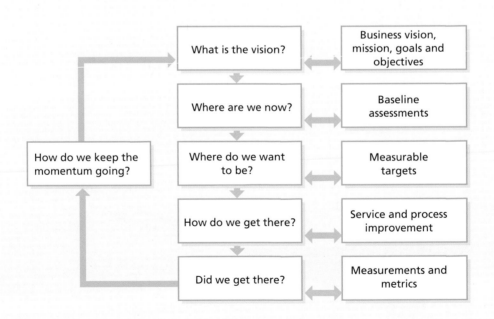

Figure 8.2 Continual service improvement approach

- Assess the current situation to obtain an accurate, unbiased snapshot of where the organization is right now. This baseline assessment is an analysis of the current position in terms of the business, organization, people, process and technology.

- Understand and agree on the priorities for improvement based on a deeper development of the principles defined in the vision. The full vision may be years away but this step provides specific goals and a manageable timeframe.

- Detail the CSI plan to achieve higher-quality service provision by implementing or improving IT service management processes.

- Verify that measurements and metrics are in place and that the milestones were achieved, process compliance is high, and business objectives and priorities were met by the level of service.

- Finally, the approach should ensure that the momentum for quality improvement is maintained by assuring that changes become embedded in the organization.

The business needs to be involved with continual service improvement in decision-making on what improvement initiatives make sense and add the greatest value back to the business. There are some key questions that will assist the business in making decisions about whether a CSI initiative is warranted or not:

- What is the vision?
- Where are we now?
- Where do we want to be?
- How do we get there?
- Did we get there?

8.4.3 Measurement

8.4.3.1 Vision to measurements

Metrics define what is to be measured. Metrics are usually specialized by the subject area, in which case they are valid only within a certain domain and cannot be directly benchmarked or interpreted outside it. Generic metrics, however, can be aggregated across subject areas or business units of an enterprise. Figure 8.3 shows the full hierarchy from the business vision through to measurements.

A **vision** is a description of what an organization intends to become in the future.

The **mission statement** of an organization is a short but complete description of the overall purpose and intentions of that organization. It states what is to be achieved, but not how this should be done.

A **goal** is a means to help us to decide on a course of action.

The **objective** is the defined purpose or aim of a process, an activity or an organization as a whole. Objectives are usually expressed as measurable targets.

A **critical success factor** (CSF) is something that must happen if a process, project, plan or service is to succeed. It is recommended that a service or process has no more than two to five CSFs associated with it at any given time.

A **key performance indicator** (KPI) is a metric that is used to help manage a process, service or activity. Many metrics may be measured, but only the most important of these are defined as KPIs and used actively to manage and report on the process, service or activity. KPIs are used to measure the achievement of each CSF. For example, a CSF of 'protect IT services when making changes'

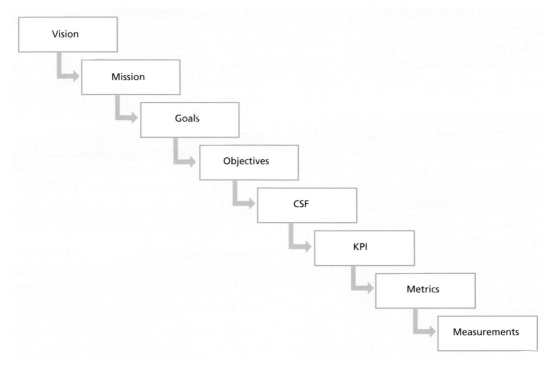

Figure 8.3 From vision to measurements

could be measured by KPIs such as 'percentage reduction of unsuccessful changes', 'percentage reduction in changes causing incidents' etc.

It is recommended that no more than two to five KPIs are defined per CSF at any given time. Based on what is important to the business and IT management, the KPIs may change over a period of time.

A **metric** is something that is measured and reported to help manage a process, service or activity. In general, a metric is a scale of measurement defined in terms of a standard, i.e. in terms of a well-defined unit.

Case study: service management in practice (Brigitte's experience)

When the hotel grew from a small family-run hotel to a larger hotel, the owner realized that he was losing his close relationship with all the hotel guests and employees, and he no longer knew enough about their needs and opinions to make the right decisions.

As a result the owner started to ask for information such as: 'I want a weekly report on the number of guests we have had and how many nights they stayed.' More and more reports were made until one day he realized that the hotel was spending a considerable amount of time making reports that were seldom or never used.

He decided to take a more structured approach to reporting:

- First he identified the ideal subjects to measure and report on. The list was quite long.
- Then he identified subjects to be measured from a practical point of view: what could be measured without too much work. Not all measurements were equally important. Some subjects required constant measuring, e.g. the number of guests/nights. Other subjects would be measured from time to time, for example the guest satisfaction with cleaning – this was measured before and after changes in the cleaning standard and in one week every year (chosen randomly).
- Then it was just hard work, collecting the data, analysing it and acting on the outcome of the analysis.
- Once every six months the owner evaluates whether the most beneficial subjects are measured; if they are not, he sets up a new report and measurement requirement.

8.4.3.2 Baselines

An important starting point for highlighting improvement is to establish baselines as markers or starting points for later comparison. Baselines are also used to establish an initial data point to determine whether a service or process needs to be improved.

If a baseline is not initially established, the first measurement efforts will become the baseline. This is why it is essential to collect data at the outset, even if the integrity of the data is in question. It is better to have data to question than to have no data at all.

8.4.3.3 Types of metrics

It is important to remember that there are three types of metrics that an organization will need to collect to support CSI activities.

Technology metrics

These metrics are often associated with component-based and application-based metrics, such as performance, availability etc.

Process metrics

These metrics are captured in the form of critical success factors (CSFs), key performance indicators (KPIs) and activity metrics for the service management processes. These metrics can help to determine the overall health of a process. Four key questions that KPIs can help to answer concern quality, performance, value and compliance in following the process. Continual service improvement uses these metrics as input in identifying improvement opportunities for each process.

Service metrics

These metrics are the results of the end-to-end service. Component metrics can be used to compute the service metrics.

8.5 PROCESSES

The ITIL Foundation syllabus covers one continual service improvement process: the seven-step improvement process.

8.5.1 The seven-step improvement process

This process is responsible for defining and managing the steps needed to identify, define, gather, process, analyse, present and implement improvements. The performance of the IT service provider is continually measured by this process, and improvements are made to processes, IT services and IT infrastructure in order to increase efficiency and effectiveness.

8.5.1.1 Purpose and objectives

The purpose of the seven-step improvement process is to define and manage the steps needed to identify, define, gather, process, analyse, present and implement improvements.

The objectives of the seven-step improvement process are to:

- Identify opportunities for improving services, processes, tools etc.
- Reduce the cost of providing services and ensure that IT services enable the required business outcomes to be achieved.
- Identify what needs to be measured, analysed and reported to establish improvement opportunities.
- Continually review service achievements to ensure that they remain matched to business requirements, and continually align and re-align service provision with outcome requirements.
- Understand what to measure, why it is being measured and carefully define the successful outcome.

8.5.1.2 Scope

The seven-step improvement process includes analysis of the performance and capabilities of services, processes throughout the lifecycle, partners and technology.

It includes the continual alignment of the portfolio of IT services with the current and future business needs as well as the maturity of the enabling IT processes for each service.

It also includes making best use of the technology that the organization has and looks to exploit new technology as it becomes available where there is a business case for doing so.

Also within the scope are the organizational structure, the capabilities of the personnel, and asking whether people are working in appropriate functions and roles, and if they have the required skills.

8.5.1.3 Basic concepts

The CSI register

It is likely that several initiatives or possibilities for improvement will be identified. It is recommended that a continual service improvement (CSI) register is kept to record all the improvement opportunities. The CSI register provides a coordinated, consistent view of the potentially numerous improvement activities. Each activity should be categorized into small, medium or large undertakings as well as initiatives that can be achieved quickly, or in the medium term or longer term.

> **Definition**
>
> A **continual service improvement (CSI) register** is a database or structured document used to record and manage improvement opportunities throughout their lifecycle.

It is important to define the interface from the CSI register of initiatives to strategic initiatives and to processes such as problem management, capacity management and change management.

8.5.1.4 Process activities

The key activities within the seven-step improvement process (as illustrated in Figure 8.4) are:

- **Identify the strategy for improvement** Identify the overall vision, business need, the strategy and the tactical and operational goals.

- **Define what you will measure** Service strategy and service design should have identified this information early in the lifecycle. Continual service improvement (CSI) can then start its cycle all over again at 'Where are we now?' and 'Where do we want to be?' This identifies the ideal situation for both the business and IT.

CSI can conduct a gap analysis to identify the opportunities for improvement as well as answering the question 'How do we get there?'

- **Gather the data** In order to properly answer the question 'Did we get there?', data must first be gathered. Data can be gathered from many different sources based on goals and objectives identified. At this point the data is raw and no conclusions are drawn.

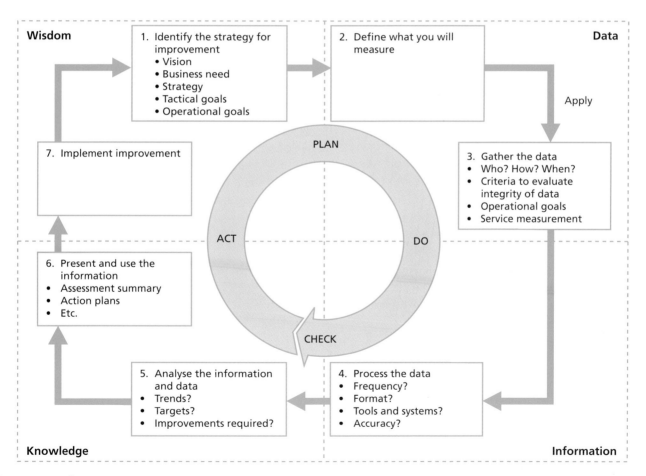

Figure 8.4 The seven-step improvement process

■ **Process the data** Here the data is processed in alignment with the critical success factors (CSFs) and key performance indicators (KPIs) specified. This means that timeframes are coordinated, unaligned data is rationalized and made consistent, and gaps in the data are identified. Once we have rationalized the data we can begin analysis.

■ **Analyse the information and data** As we bring the data more and more into context, it evolves from raw data into information with which we can start to answer questions about who, what, when, where and how as well as trends and the impact on the business.

■ **Present and use the information** Here the answer to 'Did we get there?' is formatted and communicated in whatever way necessary to present to the various stakeholders an accurate picture of the results of the improvement efforts. Knowledge is presented to the business in a form and manner that reflects their needs and assists them in determining the next steps.

■ **Implement improvement** The knowledge gained is used to optimize, improve and correct services and processes. Issues have been identified and now solutions are implemented – wisdom is applied to the knowledge. Following this step, the organization establishes a new baseline and the cycle begins anew.

Figure 8.4 also shows how the cycle fits into the Data-to-Information-to-Knowledge-to-Wisdom (DIKW) structure of knowledge management. The integration of the Plan-Do-Check-Act (PDCA) cycle and the seven-step improvement process is as follows:

■ Plan
  ● Identify the strategy for improvement
  ● Define what you will measure
■ Do
  ● Gather the data
  ● Process the data
■ Check
  ● Analyse the information and data
  ● Present and use the information
■ Act
  ● Implement improvement.

While these seven steps appear to form a circular set of activities, in fact they constitute a knowledge spiral. In practice, knowledge gathered and wisdom derived from the knowledge at one level of the organization becomes a data input to the next.

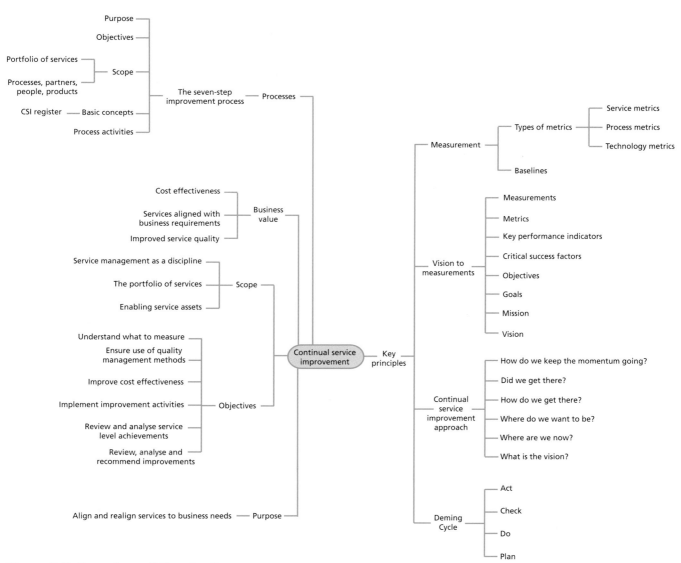

Figure 8.5 Overview of Chapter 8

8.6   SAMPLE QUESTIONS

1   What is contained within the 'Do' stage of the Deming Cycle?

a   A gap analysis is performed and the steps for closing the gaps defined

b   The actual implementation of the improvement initiative, and establishment of the smooth operation of the process

c   Implementing the service or process improvements and establishing whether further work is necessary to close any remaining gaps

d   Monitoring, measuring and reviewing the services and service management processes that were targeted for improvement

2   When using the seven-step improvement process, which of the following pieces of information is useful when determining the strategy for improvement?

1   Organizational vision

2   Incident management data

3   Problem management data

4   Strategy of the organization

a   1 and 4 only

b   2 and 3 only

c   None of the above

d   All of the above

3   In the continual service improvement approach, once all the measurements and metrics have been collated to confirm that the desired end result has been achieved, what activity should then take place?

a   In order to close off the improvement activity a confirmation of achievement of the business case should follow

b   Capture the baseline assessments so that they can be used for later comparison

c   Agree what needs to occur to ensure that the momentum for quality improvement is maintained

d   Understand the high-level business objectives to ensure that the vision has been captured

4   Which of the following is NOT a type of metric which can be used to support continual service improvement activities?

a   Service metrics

b   Technology metrics

c   Process metrics

d   Critical success factor (CSF) metrics

5   What is the MAIN purpose of the CSI register?

a   To capture a baseline for future opportunities

b   To record all key performance indicators for each process

c   To give visibility to, and to record all improvement opportunities

d   To log all changes resulting from service improvement initiatives

Service management technology

9 Service management technology

Technology plays a major role in service management, and mechanisms for maintaining and maximizing benefit from that technology must be in place.

To support the development and management of new or changed services, the hotel has a tool for release management of the restaurant menu and a tool for release management of new work instructions. To make sure that changes actually work, the hotel also has a tool for managing requirements and testing new equipment. Especially in the new conference centre, video equipment, wireless internet connection, pens and coffee machines have to be tested often.

9.1 USE OF TECHNOLOGY

Service management technology enables communication between service providers and customers. There are five modes in which technology interacts with a service provider's customers (see Figure 9.1):

- **Technology-free** Technology is not involved in the service provision.
- **Technology-assisted** Only the service provider has access to the technology.
- **Technology-facilitated** Both the service provider and the customer have access to the same technology.
- **Technology-mediated** The service provider and the customer are not in physical proximity.
- **Technology-generated** The service provider is represented entirely by technology, commonly known as self-service.

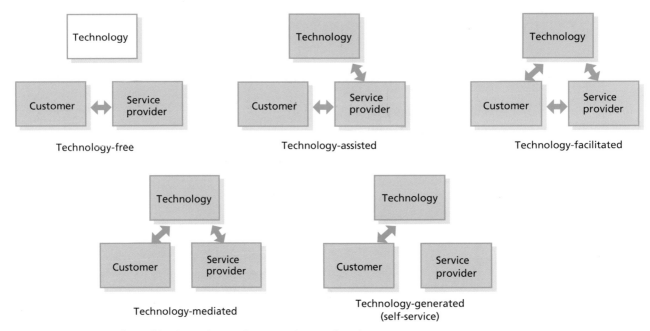

Figure 9.1 Five modes of interaction using service technology

9.2 SERVICE AUTOMATION

Automation should be considered to improve the utility and warranty of services.

9.2.1 Reasons for automation

Automation may offer advantages in many areas of opportunity, including the following:

- The capacity of automated resources can be more easily adjusted in response to variations in demand volumes.
- Automated resources can handle capacity with fewer restrictions on time of access.
- Automated systems present a good basis for measuring and improving service processes by holding constant the factor of human resources.
- Many optimization problems, such as scheduling, routing and allocation of resources, require computing power that is beyond the capacity of human agents.
- Automation is a means of capturing the knowledge required for a service process.

The following are some of the areas where service management can benefit from automation:

- Design and modelling
- Service catalogue
- Pattern recognition and analysis
- Classification, prioritization and routing
- Detection and monitoring
- Optimization.

9.2.2 Preparing for automation

Applying automation randomly can create more problems or worsen existing ones. The following guidelines should be applied:

- Simplify the service processes before automating them.
- Clarify the flow of activities, allocation of tasks, need for information, and interactions.
- In self-service situations, reduce the amount of contact that users have with the underlying systems and processes.
- Do not be in a hurry to automate tasks and interactions that are neither simple nor routine in terms of inputs, resources and outcomes.

9.3   SERVICE ANALYTICS

Information is static. It only becomes knowledge when placed in the context of patterns and their implications. Those patterns give a high level of predictability and reliability on how the data will change over time. By understanding patterns of information, we can answer 'How?' questions such as:

- How does this incident affect the service?
- How is the business impacted?
- How do we respond?

This is service analytics.

Service analytics is useful for modelling existing infrastructure components and support services to the higher-level business services. Infrastructure events are then tied to corresponding business processes. The component-to-system-to-process linkage – also known as the service model – allows us to clearly identify the business impact of an event.

Instead of responding to discrete events, managers can characterize the behaviour of a service. This behaviour is then compared with a baseline of the normal behaviour for that time of day or business cycle.

With service analytics, not only can an operations group do a better job of identifying and correcting problems from the user's standpoint, but it can also predict the impact of changes to the environment. This same model can be turned around to show business demand for IT services. This is a high leverage point when building a dynamic provisioning or on-demand environment.

9.4   SAMPLE QUESTIONS

1   Which of the following are advantages of automation?

   1   The capacity of automated resources can be more easily adjusted

   2   Automation presents a good basis for measuring and improving service processes

   3   Many activities require computing power that is beyond the power of human agents

   4   Automation can be a means for capturing the knowledge required for a service process

      a   1 and 2 only

      b   1, 2 and 3 only

      c   3 and 4 only

      d   All of the above

2   When the customer is supported by technology alone from its service provider, this is known as what?

      a   Discovery technology

      b   Remote support

      c   Self-service

      d   Diagnostic utilities

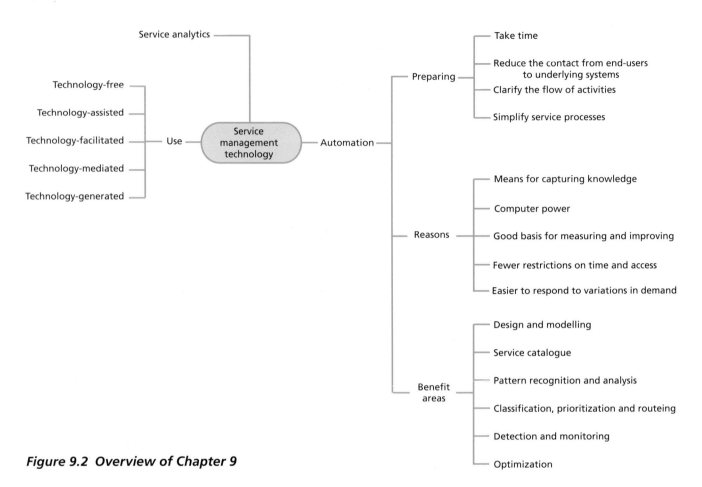

Figure 9.2 Overview of Chapter 9

How it all fits together

10

10 How it all fits together

Each lifecycle stage is dependent on input from and provides output to the other stages in the lifecycle.

10.1 INTEGRATION ACROSS THE SERVICE LIFECYCLE

Stages of the lifecycle work together as an integrated system to support the ultimate objective of service management for business value realization. Every stage is interdependent as shown in Figure 10.1.

The service knowledge management system (SKMS) enables integration across the service lifecycle stages. It provides secure and controlled access to the knowledge, information and data that are needed to manage and deliver services. The service portfolio represents all the assets presently engaged or being released in various stages of the lifecycle.

Figure 10.1 gives a good overview of the links, inputs and outputs involved at each stage of the service lifecycle. It illustrates the key outputs produced by each stage, which are used as inputs by the subsequent stages.

10.2 SPECIALIZATION AND COORDINATION

Organizations need a collaborative approach for the management of assets which are used to deliver and support services for their customers.

Organizations should function in the same manner as a high-performing sports team. Each player in a team, and each member of the team's organization who is not a player, position themselves to support the goal of the team. Each player and team member has a different specialization that contributes to the whole. The team matures over time, taking into account feedback from experience, best practice, current process and procedures to become an agile high-performing team.

Specialization and coordination are necessary in the lifecycle approach. Specialization allows for expert focus on components of the service, but components of the service also need to work together for value. Specialization combined with coordination helps to manage expertise, improve focus and reduce overlaps and gaps in processes. Specialization and coordination together help to create a collaborative and agile organizational architecture that maximizes utilization of assets.

Coordination across the lifecycle creates an environment focused on business and customer outcomes instead of just IT objectives and projects. Coordination is also essential between functional groups, across the value network, and between processes and technology.

10.3 MONITORING AND CONTROL

Each activity in a service management process should be monitored. The role of operational monitoring and control is to ensure that the process or service performs exactly as specified, which is why monitoring and control are primarily concerned with maintaining the status quo.

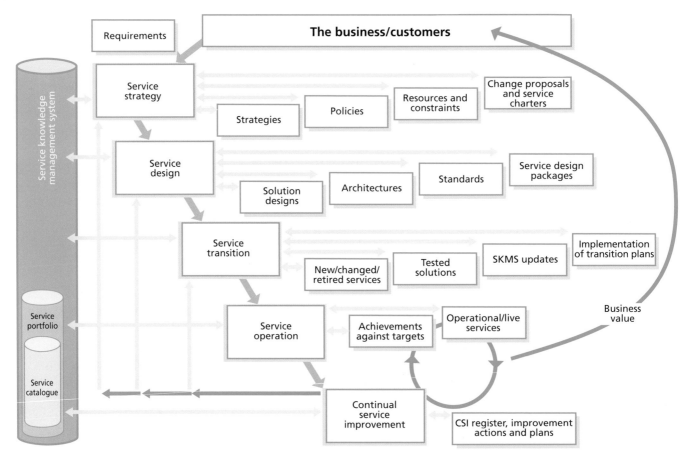

Figure 10.1 Integration across the service lifecycle

Figure 10.2 illustrates the monitoring and control of a process or of the components used to deliver a service.

The norms and monitoring and control mechanisms are defined in service design, but they are based on the standards and architectures defined during service strategy.

Notice that the second level of monitoring in this monitor-and-control loop is performed by the CSI processes through service strategy and service design. These relationships are represented by the numbered arrows on the figure as follows:

- **Arrow 1** In this case CSI has recognized that the service will be improved by making a change to the service strategy. This could be a result of the business needing a change to the service portfolio, or the realization that the architecture does not deliver what was expected.
- **Arrow 2** In this case the service level requirements need to be adjusted. It could be that the service is too expensive or that operations management is unable to maintain service quality in the current architecture.

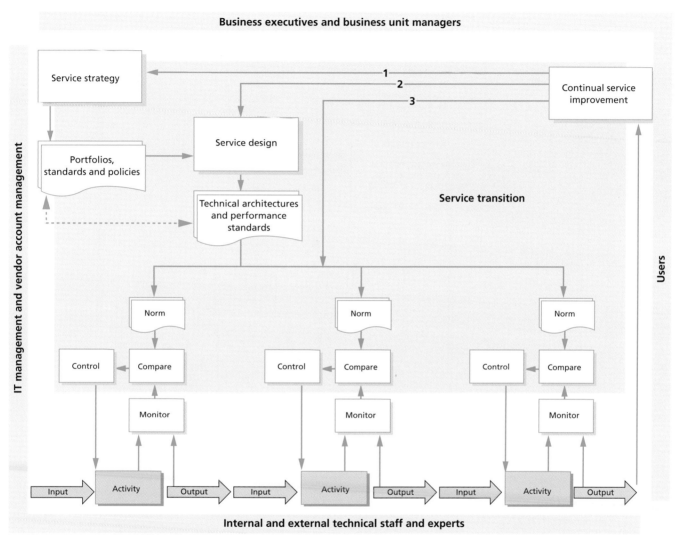

Figure 10.2 Monitoring and control across the service lifecycle

■ **Arrow 3** In this case the norms specified in service design are not being adhered to. This could be because they are not appropriate or executable, or because of a lack of education or communication. The norms and the lack of compliance need to be investigated and action taken to rectify the situation.

Service transition provides a major set of checks and balances in these processes. It does so as follows:

■ For new services, service transition will ensure that the technical architectures are appropriate and that the operational performance standards can be executed.

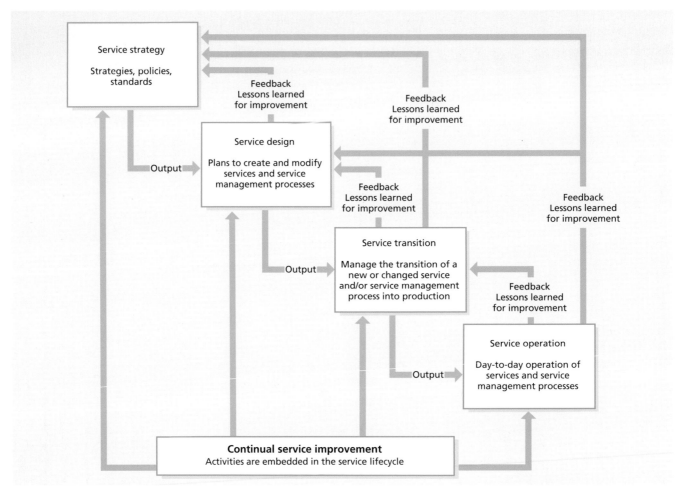

Figure 10.3 Continual service improvement and the service lifecycle

■ For existing services, change management will manage any of the changes that are required as part of a control (e.g. tuning), as well as any changes represented by the arrows labelled 1, 2 and 3. Although service transition does not define strategy and design services per se, it provides coordination and assurance that the services are working, and will continue to work, as planned.

10.4 CONTINUAL SERVICE IMPROVEMENT

The strength of the service lifecycle rests upon continual feedback throughout each stage of the lifecycle. This feedback ensures that service improvement is managed from a business perspective and is measured in terms of the value the business derives from services at any point in time during the service lifecycle. The service lifecycle is non-linear in design. At every point in the service lifecycle, the process of monitoring, assessment and feedback between each stage drives decisions about the need for minor course corrections or major service improvement initiatives.

Figure 10.3 illustrates some examples of the continual feedback system built into the service lifecycle.

An IT service provider does not need to wait until a service or service management process is transitioned into the operations area to begin identifying improvement opportunities.

The examination and exam preparation

11

11 The examination and exam preparation

11.1 THE EXAMINATION

The examination is a closed-book paper consisting of 40 multiple-choice questions. All 40 questions should be attempted. Each question has four choices, and the candidate must select one of these to answer a question. Only one of the choices is correct.

The examination can be taken either on paper or online.

A maximum of 60 minutes is allowed to answer the paper. Candidates completing an exam in a language that is not their mother tongue and where the language of the exam is not their primary business language have a maximum of 75 minutes to complete the exam and are allowed the use of a dictionary.

Candidates must answer 26 or more questions correctly to pass the examination, corresponding to a pass score of 65%.

Candidates who fail may retake the examination. There is no limit to the number of times a candidate may re-sit the examination.

11.2 EXAM PREPARATION

Attending an accredited Foundation training course is strongly recommended but is not a prerequisite to sitting the examination. Candidates should note that the overall public examination pass rates are notably lower than the rates for candidates who have attended an accredited training course. Candidates are recommended to study for a total of at least three days prior to the exam.

You should start preparing for the examination from the first day of the course. Use an effective note-taking system, and review the course material regularly. Transfer information to be learned onto note cards and review them every day.

Homework and self-study will be expected. Make appointments with yourself (and your surroundings) for study time.

Practise taking the examination to help familiarize yourself with it. You can use the sample tests in this publication, and your training provider will also provide you with recent sample papers. Because the examination is a timed test, you should prepare for your upcoming exam under similar conditions. Make sure that whenever you take practice tests, you time yourself using the same amount of allotted time that will be allowed on the real test. Know in advance how many minutes you can spend per question, and every few questions check against the clock to see how you are doing.

Prepare far enough in advance so that you can actually relax the night before the exam.

During the examination:

- Read each question carefully to make sure you understand the type of answer required.
- Come up with the answer in your head before looking at the possible answers.
- Read and consider all of the answer choices before you choose the option that best responds to the question.

- Make sure you answer the question that is being asked.
- There will be no trick questions so do not waste time and energy looking for catch questions.
- Answer the easy questions first, then go back and answer the more difficult ones.
- When attempting difficult questions, eliminate as many incorrect answers as you can, then make an educated guess from among those remaining.
- Do not spend too much time on any one question.
- Check that you have answered every question. Your scores on the multiple-choice tests are based on the number of questions you answer correctly. There is no penalty for guessing.
- Review your work. If you finish a test before time is up, go back and check your work.
- Do not keep on changing an answer – usually your first choice is the right one, unless you misread the question.

Sample ITIL Foundation examination

12 Sample ITIL Foundation examination

12.1 INSTRUCTIONS

All 40 questions should be attempted.

There are no trick questions.

You have 60 minutes to complete this paper. Candidates completing an exam in a language that is not their mother tongue and where the language of the exam is not their primary business language have a maximum of 75 minutes and are allowed the use of a dictionary.

You must get 26 or more answers correct to pass.

12.2 QUESTIONS

1   Which process has PRIMARY responsibility for establishing and maintaining the relationship between the service provider and its customer?

   a   Problem management

   b   Change management

   c   Business relationship management

   d   Service portfolio management

2   Which of the following is NOT within the scope of problem management?

   a   To assess the impact and urgency of incident tickets

   b   To determine resolution for underlying issues

   c   Implementation of resolution through the correct control procedures

   d   Pro-active identification of recurring incidents

3   Which of the following would be an appropriate type of service level agreement?

   a   Contract level

   b   Technology level

   c   Corporate level

   d   Operational level

4   Which of the following roles would be valid members of a change advisory board (CAB) meeting?

   1   Suppliers

   2   Change manager

   3   Service owner

   4   Release manager

      a   1, 2 and 3 only

      b   2, 3 and 4 only

      c   2 and 4 only

      d   All of the above

5   What is the main activity used to help the IT service provider understand and plan for a workload profile?

   a   Developing the requirements for service utility

   b   Providing the appropriate value from the service level package

   c   Understanding the value that IT needs to give to the business

   d   Understanding patterns of business activity

6   Which of the following are the main objectives for the service desk?

   1   To provide management information

   2   To restore normal service to the users as quickly as possible

   3   To manage the incident through its lifecycle

   4   To prevent problems and resulting incidents from happening

      a   1, 2 and 4 only

      b   3 and 4 only

      c   1, 2 and 3 only

      d   All of the above

7   Who is accountable for ensuring that a process is performing to the agreed standards?

   a   The process manager

   b   The process owner

   c   The service owner

   d   The process practitioner

8   Which of the following is the BEST description of an internal service?

   a   A service providing a value but taking away the ownership of risk and cost for the customer

   b   A service delivered between departments in the same organization

   c   A service delivered to customers who are not directly part of the organization

   d   A service not directly used by the business but required to provide the overall service

9   Which of the following statements BEST describes the difference between an operational level agreement (OLA) and an underpinning contract (UC)?

   a   The OLA is an underpinning agreement with legally binding terms whereas the UC supports the SLA, and is therefore not formal

   b   The OLA is an internal document that defines the working relationship between different groups within the service provider organization whereas the UC is a legally binding document for a supplier in support of the SLA

   c   The UC defines targets and responsibilities that are required to meet agreed service level targets in a service level agreement, whereas the OLA describes best endeavours for a service

   d   There are no differences between a UC and an OLA as they both support the SLA

10   There are five aspects of a successful service design stage. Which aspect is missing from the list below?

   1   The design of the management information systems and tools

   2   The design of the technology and management architectures

   3   The design of the processes

   4   The design of the measurement methods and metrics

      a   The design of the service design package (SDP)

      b   The design of the documentation

c   The design of the service solution

d   The design of the business processes

11   Which of the following is the CORRECT definition of a business case?

a   The decision support and planning tool to predict the costs associated with the implementation of a new service

b   A justification for a significant item of expenditure, which will include information about costs, benefits, options, risks and possible problems

c   The quantification of the costs of each service and how each service is consumed

d   The documentation which demonstrates the visibility and accountability of each business unit

12   The release package is an output from which phase of the service lifecycle?

a   Service strategy

b   Service design

c   Service transition

d   Service operation

13   Which of the following functions has a key objective to provide the technical expertise and specialized resources for the overall IT infrastructure, throughout the service lifecycle?

a   Technical management

b   IT operations

c   Incident management

d   Applications management

14   Which of the following are valid service provider types?

1   A centralized services unit

2   An internal service provider

3   An external service provider

4   A shared services unit

a   1 and 4 only

b   2 and 3 only

c   2, 3 and 4 only

d   All of the above

15   Which of the following is NOT within the scope of the design coordination process?

a   Maintenance of policies and standards for the service design activities

b   Assistance and support of projects through the service design stage

c   Management of any conflict for resources

d   Assurance that both utility and warranty are tested

16   In order to optimize the efficiency of the change process, many low-risk routine changes may be categorized as pre-authorized by change management. What type of change is this known as?

a   A service request

b   A change request

c   A normal change

d   A standard change

17 What is contained within the definitive media library?

a Secure definitive authorized versions of both software and media CIs that have passed quality assurance checks

b The relationship model of all service assets, infrastructure and individual components that make up a service

c Secure definitive authorized versions of both software and media CIs that are waiting to pass quality assurance checks

d Secure backup tapes

18 In which information source would you find a complete list of current improvement opportunities and their benefits?

a The continual service improvement (CSI) register

b A service improvement plan

c The business case

d The configuration management system (CMS)

19 Which of the following is the BEST description of why ITIL is so successful?

a ITIL has now been followed for more than 30 years, ensuring that risks are minimized and value is achieved in organizations

b ITIL represents a common framework of practices that unite all areas of IT service provision to deliver value to the business

c ITIL represents a proven methodology that provides an end-to-end delivery of quality services and value to the business

d ITIL is recognized as a worldwide standard of conformance to best practice that ensures that everyone in the organization uses the same terms and standards

20 Which of the following is the first stage of the seven-step improvement process?

a Define what you will measure

b Identify the strategy for improvement

c Check the integrity of the data to be used for analysis

d Determine the baseline

21 Which of the following are key elements that need to be defined as part of a process?

1 The activities contained within the process

2 The process policy

3 Roles within the organization that will need to carry out the process

4 Appropriate metrics for the process

a 1, 2 and 3 only

b 3 and 4 only

c 1, 2 and 4 only

d All of the above

22 Which element of the DIKW model can NOT be supported by automation?

a Data

b Information

c Knowledge

d Wisdom

23 What is the MAIN purpose of service transition planning and support?

a To control the assets required to deliver the services to the organization, and ensure that accurate and reliable information is available

b To provide overall planning for service transition and coordinate the resources that they require

c To provide overall planning and guidance for all projects as they transition into service operation

d To identify, manage and control risks to minimize any adverse impact and disruption on service operation

24 Which of the following tasks is IT operations NOT responsible for?

a Incident resolution

b Managing applications throughout their lifecycle

c Managing the facilities environment

d Monitoring events

25 During the incident management process the service desk is often unable to resolve the incident themselves so they would escalate the incident to another specialist team. What type of escalation is this known as?

a Functional

b Hierarchic

c Problem management

d Call closure

26 What type of categorization would be assigned to a supplier if they are providing a service that has medium risk and impact to the business and medium value and importance?

a Commodity supplier

b Operational supplier

c Tactical supplier

d Strategic supplier

27 Which of the following are appropriate examples of a service request?

1 A password change or reset

2 A minor code change request from a user to modify a particular application

3 The relocation of some desktop equipment

4 A question requesting information

a 1, 2 and 3 only

b 2, and 4 only

c 1, 3 and 4 only

d All of the above

28 Which of the following is the PRIMARY process for which a business impact analysis is required?

a Service level management

b Financial management

c IT service continuity management

d Request fulfilment

29 Which of the following is a key guideline when preparing for automation?

   a Amend the processes to reflect the tool

   b Evaluate quality tools on the market

   c Simplify the service processes

   d Review any complicated tasks first

30 In which stage of the service lifecycle is governance established?

   a Service strategy

   b Service design

   c Service transition

   d Continual service improvement

31 Which functional group will normally take action on events?

   a Incident management

   b IT operations

   c Service desk

   d Problem management

32 Which of the following are key elements that should be included within the service design package (SDP)?

   1 Business requirements

   2 Organizational readiness assessment

   3 Testing plan

   4 Service acceptance criteria

      a 1, 2 and 4 only

      b 2 and 4 only

      c 1, 2 and 3 only

      d All of the above

33 Which of the following is the CORRECT sequence of activities during the incident lifecycle after the incident has been identified?

   a 1 – Initial diagnosis and possible escalation. 2 – Incident categorization. 3 – Incident logging. 4 – Incident prioritization. 5 – Investigation and diagnosis. 6 – Incident closure. 7 – Resolution and recovery.

   b 1 – Incident logging. 2 – Incident prioritization. 3 – Initial diagnosis and possible escalation. 4 – Investigation and diagnosis. 5 – Resolution and recovery. 6 – Incident categorization. 7 – Incident closure.

   c 1 – Incident categorization. 2 – Incident logging. 3 – Incident prioritization. 4 – Initial diagnosis and possible escalation. 5 – Investigation and diagnosis. 6 – Resolution and recovery. 7 – Incident closure.

   d 1 – Incident logging. 2 – Incident categorization. 3 – Incident prioritization. 4 – Initial diagnosis and possible escalation. 5 – Investigation and diagnosis. 6 – Resolution and recovery. 7 – Incident closure.

34 Which of the following will give an overall view of the periodic reports showing performance against all SLA targets?

   a OLA chart

   b SLAM chart

   c RAG status

   d Underpinning contract performance

35 Which of the following is the PRIMARY objective of access management?

a To provide the right for users to be able to use a service at all times to support their business processes

b To align IT security with business security and ensure that it is effectively managed

c To provide the appropriate right for users to be able to use a service or group of services

d To ensure that IT services can be resumed in the event of a disaster, within required and agreed business timescales

36 To answer the question 'Where are we now?' in the continual service approach, we need to know:

a How we will keep the momentum going

b The current baseline assessments

c The business vision

d The new measurement targets

37 Which service lifecycle publication provides guidance on testing?

a *ITIL Service Operation*

b *ITIL Service Transition*

c *ITIL Service Design*

d *ITIL Service Strategy*

38 Which service operation function would contribute to the decision on whether to buy off-the-shelf software packages to support the business processes?

a The service desk

b Technical management

c Application management

d IT operations

39 Which of the following statements is the CORRECT definition for warranty?

a The delivery of positive attributes of a service

b The service is assured, and no risks will be introduced into live services

c The service is fit for purpose

d The service will meet its agreed requirements

40 Which of the following activities would NOT be completed as part of the change management process?

a Planning and controlling the change

b Management reporting for change

c Change decision-making and authorization

d Applying a fix for an emergency change

Answers **13**

13 Answers

CHAPTER 2 INTRODUCTION TO SERVICE MANAGEMENT

1   b – Option (c) and option (d) describe a process characteristic. Option (a) partially describes a function but it would not just cover a single task. Definition of a function: a team or group of people and the tools they use to carry out one or more processes or activities (see section 2.2.2).

2   b – RACI is an acronym for 'Responsible', 'Accountable', 'Consulted' and 'Informed' (see section 2.2.3.1).

3   c – Except for option (a), which is the responsibility of the process owner, the rest of the activities do form part of the responsibilities of a process practitioner (see section 2.2.3.5).

4   b – Option (a) describes the roles within service operation; option (c) misses components related to external suppliers; and option (d) describes a responsibility of the service level manager. Definition of service owner role: a role which is accountable for a specific service within an organization, regardless of where the underpinning technology components, processes or professional capabilities reside (see section 2.2.3.2).

5   c – Option (a) describes an internal service; option (b) describes an external service; and (d) relates to a type of service provider (Type I) (see section 2.1.2).

CHAPTER 4 SERVICE STRATEGY

1   a – The service design package is produced and is an output from service design (see section 4.1).

2   c – All elements in (a), (b) and (c) are valid elements: 'Value needs to be defined in terms of three areas: the business outcomes achieved, the customer's preferences and the customer's perception of what was delivered' (*ITIL Service Strategy*, 2011, section 3.2.3). In option (d) merely understanding risk would not be a value driver (see section 4.4.1).

3   c – Any service item not yet in operational services should be contained in the pipeline; option (a), the service catalogue, is for live operational services; and option (b) is for services that are retiring and will no longer be used by customers (see section 4.4.3).

4   c – NOT option 4 – this would be done following the business case being approved. Definition of business case: Justification for a significant item of expenditure (see section 4.4.5).

CHAPTER 5 SERVICE DESIGN

1 b – The organizational structure would be decided during the service strategy stage (see sections 4.1 and 5.1).

2 b – Option (a) is incorrect as this describes a service provider; option (c) is the definition of an OLA; and option (d) refers to transitioning services from project teams. Definition of SLA: an agreement between an IT service provider and a customer (see section 5.5.3.3).

3 a – The partners responsible are not an aspect of service design. The five service design aspects are the service solution; the management information systems; the technology and management architecture (b); the processes required (d); and the measurement methods and metrics (c) (see section 5.4.2).

4 d – The purpose of design coordination is 'to ensure the goals and objectives of the service design stage are met by providing and maintaining a single point of coordination and control for all activities and processes'. Option (a) describes the process that provides the planning and management of capabilities and resources for service transition; options (b) SLM and (c) risk management are process activities that would be carried out in service design (see section 5.5.1).

5 a – Reliability is a measure of how long a service component or configuration item can perform to its agreed function without interruption; (b) describes maintainability; (c) is when a service is unavailable; and (d) is the supplier's ability to restore service (see section 5.5.5.3).

CHAPTER 6 SERVICE TRANSITION

1 c – Option 4 would be carried out by the business itself, as IT would only be indirectly involved with the training activities for the actual business operational change (see section 6.1).

2 a – All items are valid elements that could be contained within the SKMS (see section 6.5.5.3 and Figure 6.7).

3 a – Option (b) is describing a configuration item; option (c) describes the SKMS; and option (d) is only partially accurate – the CMS does not have to be a single repository. Definition of CMS: a set of tools, data and information that is used to support service asset and configuration management (see section 6.5.2.3).

4 b – Remediation is used to ensure that appropriate action can be taken to recover after a failed change or release; (a) ITSC invocation is not always necessary following a failed change; (c) an emergency change is not always necessary; (d) describes a change model (see section 6.5.3.3).

5 d – A change proposal is used to communicate a high-level description of a major change (see section 6.5.3.3).

6 b – This is the correct sequence. Option (a) refers to Deming's Plan-Do-Check-Act cycle for continuous improvement (see section 6.5.4.4).

CHAPTER 7 SERVICE OPERATION

1   c – Option (a) is an objective of service design; option (b) is an objective of service transition; and option (d) is a small part of the coverage of service operation (see section 7.1).

2   c – Option (a) the process owner is accountable for the process; option (b) the service desk is responsible for the incident through its lifecycle, but all teams will have to take responsibility for the process if they are dealing with incidents (see section 7.6).

3   a – Option (b) problem management may get involved in major incidents, but it is the responsibility of incident management to manage a major incident, (c) is an objective of incident management, and option (d) although problem management is responsible for providing a workaround, it is not a key purpose and also not always possible to do (see section 7.5.4.1).

4   d – An incident should only ever be raised when there has been a degradation of service, whether the customer is aware of it or not (see section 7.5.1.3).

5   c – A technical service desk is not a valid description for a service desk (see section 7.6.1.3).

6   b – Priority setting for an incident should be based on the impact it is having on the business and its urgency, i.e. how quickly the business needs a resolution (see section 7.5.2.3).

CHAPTER 8 CONTINUAL SERVICE IMPROVEMENT

1   b – Option (a) describes the Plan stage; option (c) describes the Act stage; and option (d) describes the activities in the Check stage (see section 8.4.1).

2   a – To identify the strategy for improvement, an organization will need its vision and strategy; incident and problem management data may be useful when data is gathered (see sections 8.5.1.1 and 8.5.1.4).

3   c – This describes the concept of 'How to keep the momentum going'. Option (a) would have taken place during the 'Did we get there?' stage; option (b) describes the data requirements at the 'Where are we now?' stage; and option (d) describes the 'What is the vision?' stage (see section 8.4.2, Figure 8.2).

4   d – A critical success factor is something that must happen if a process, project plan or service is to succeed. Metrics are used to measure the achievement of each CSF (see section 8.4.3.3).

5   c – The CSI register is a database or structured document used to record and manage improvement opportunities throughout their lifecycle. Against each item listed, the benefits that each opportunity will bring are shown. Each opportunity can be prioritized (see section 8.5.1.3).

CHAPTER 9 SERVICE MANAGEMENT TECHNOLOGY

1   d – All elements would be valid advantages of automation (see section 9.2.1).

2   c – Self-service is where the service provider is represented entirely by technology (technology-generated) (see sections 9.1 and 9.2.2).

CHAPTER 12 SAMPLE ITIL FOUNDATION EXAMINATION

1   c – Business relationship management has a primary purpose of establishing and maintaining a business relationship between the service provider and customer based on an understanding of their changing needs (see section 4.5.3.1).

2   a – Assessing impact and urgency would be within the scope of the incident management process and under the control of the service desk (see section 7.5.4.2).

3   c – There are three types of service level agreement – by service, customer-based and corporate (see section 5.5.3.3).

4   d – All roles would be valid members of a CAB including suppliers – particularly if they have changes that may impact the service (see section 6.5.3.3).

5   d – Option (a) refers to utility, and options (b) and (c) refer to other value attributes, but none of the options is associated with patterns of business activity. Definition: PBA is a workload profile of one or more business activities (see section 4.4.2).

6   c – Option 4 is a key objective for problem management (see section 7.6.1.2).

7   b – The process owner is accountable for ensuring that the process is performing to the agreed standards; (a) the process manager is accountable for the operational management of a process; (c) the service owner is accountable for the service across the lifecycle; and (d) the process practitioner is responsible for carrying out the activities within the process (see section 2.2.3.3).

8   b – Option (a) describes the definition of a service; (c) describes and external service; and (d) describes a supporting service (see section 2.1.2).

9   b – Option (a) describes the UC and OLA with the wrong and opposite meanings to the correct answer; option (c) is inaccurate, as both OLAs and UCs would have measurements set against them to determine performance in support of the SLA; option (d) suggests both are the same type of agreements. Definitions: OLA – an agreement between an IT service provider and another part of the same organization to support the delivery of the services; UC – a contract between an IT service provider and a third party (see section 5.5.3.3).

10   c – Options (a) and (b) are the outputs of the service design stage; option (d) is inaccurate as the solution should be designed to accommodate the business process (see section 5.4.2).

11 b – Option (a) suggests that is it only a planning tool; options (c) and (d) refer to financial management objectives. Definition of business case: Justification for a significant item of expenditure, which includes information about costs, benefits, options, issues, risks and possible problems (see section 4.4.5).

12 c – The release package is an output from the service transition phase (see section 6.4.1).

13 a – Option (b) IT operations provides the monitoring and control activities; (c) incident management is a process; and (d) applications management provides the technical knowledge and expertise related to the applications (see section 7.6.2.1).

14 c – Option 1 – a centralized unit is not a valid service provider type (see section 2.1.9).

15 d – Options (a), (b) and (c) are all within the scope of the design coordination process; (d) testing would be part of the service transition lifecycle phase under the process of validation and testing (see section 5.5.1.2).

16 d – Option (a) refers to the request fulfilment process; option (b) refers to the generic RFC for all changes; and option (c) refers to normal changes that should go through a formal approval process, usually via the CAB (see section 6.5.3.3).

17 a – Option (b) describes the configuration model; option (c) describes the DML in all but the fact that it is not a media library that has not passed quality assurance; and option (d) backups would not be stored in the DML. Definition of DML: one or more locations in which the definitive and authorized versions of all software CIs are securely stored. The DML may also contain associated CIs such as licences and documentation (see section 6.5.2.3).

18 a – The CSI register holds a record of all improvement opportunities, giving a structure and visibility of CSI initiatives (see section 8.5.1.3).

19 b – Option (a) ITIL is not successful just because it has been used for more than 30 years; option (c) ITIL is not a methodology; and (d) ITIL is not a standard (see section 2.3).

20 b – The first stage of the seven-step improvement process is 'identify the strategy for improvement' followed by 'define what you will measure'. Option (a) is the second stage; options (c) and (d) are not steps within the seven-step improvement process (see section 8.5.1).

21 d – All of the stated elements form part of a process as well as procedures, work instructions, triggers, input, outputs and capabilities (see section 2.2.1.1).

22 d – Wisdom cannot be replicated by automation: wisdom is the ability to make correct judgements and decisions (see section 6.5.5.3).

23 b – Option (a) describes the purpose of service asset and configuration management; option (c) relates only to projects; and (d) represents one objective of minimizing risk but this is a narrow answer (see section 6.5.1).

24 b – It is the responsibility of application management to manage applications throughout their lifecycle (see section 7.6.3.1).

25 a – Option (b) refers to the escalation of an incident up the management chain if further people need to be made aware of the incident; option (c) – incidents do not become problems just because the service desk cannot fix them; and option (d) – an incident should not be closed just because it cannot be fixed by the service desk – it would revert to a functional escalation. Definition of functional escalation: transferring an incident, problem or change to a technical team with a higher level of expertise to assist (see section 7.5.2.4).

26 c – Option (a), commodity supplier, is assigned when there is low risk and impact, and low value and importance; (b) operational supplier is the category assigned when there is either a low risk and impact or a low value and importance; and (d) strategic supplier is the category for when there is both high risk and impact and high value and importance (see section 5.5.4.3, Figure 5.5).

27 c – Option 2 would fall under the change management process and should be raised via an RFC (see section 7.5.3.3).

28 c – IT service continuity requires a BIA (see section 5.5.7.1).

29 c – Processes should be simplified first before automation (see section 9.2.2).

30 a – Governance is established in service strategy to ensure transparency and fairness on behalf of the organization (see section 4.4.6).

31 b – IT operations would normally take action on an event; (a) incident management and (d) problem management are processes not functions. The service desk (c) would not normally be responsible for events (see section 7.5.1.3).

32 d – All of the examples would be appropriate elements contained within the service design package (see section 5.4.3). Definition of SDP: a document defining all aspects of an IT service and its requirements through each stage of its lifecycle.

33 d – This is the correct sequence for the incident management process flow (see section 7.5.2.4).

34 b – A service level agreement monitoring (SLAM) chart gives an at-a-glance view of the periodic reports showing performance against all SLA targets (see section 5.5.3.3).

35 c – Option (a) access management would not grant access at all times but would very much be determined on the availability requirements that have been agreed with the business; option (b) describes the objective of information security; and option (d) describes the objective of IT service continuity (see section 7.5.5.1).

36 b – The answer to the question 'Where are we now?' involves ensuring that we have an understanding of the current performance status, which is achieved through the use of baseline assessments when we use the CSI approach (see section 8.4.2, Figure 8.2).

37 b – *ITIL Service Transition* provides guidance on testing (see section 6.2).

38   c – The application management function needs to understand the business process in order to help identify functional and manageability requirements for application software (see section 7.6.4.1).

39   d – Options (a) and (c) describe utility; option (b) covers only risk (see section 2.1.5).

40   d – Change management would not implement the fix for an emergency change – fixes are part of the incident process. It is the process of change management that would authorize the emergency change (see section 6.5.3.4).

Further information

Further information

THE OFFICIAL ITIL SERVICE MANAGEMENT PRACTICES FRAMEWORK

ITIL Service Strategy (ISBN: 9780113313044)

ITIL Service Design (ISBN: 9780113313051)

ITIL Service Transition (ISBN: 9780113313068)

ITIL Service Operation (ISBN: 9780113313075)

ITIL Continual Service Improvement
(ISBN: 9780113313082)

Introduction to the ITIL Service Lifecycle
(ISBN: 9780113313099)

USEFUL WEBSITES

ITIL
www.best-management-practice.com

www.itil-officialsite.com

Certification
www.apmgroup.co.uk

*it*SMF International
www.itsmfi.org

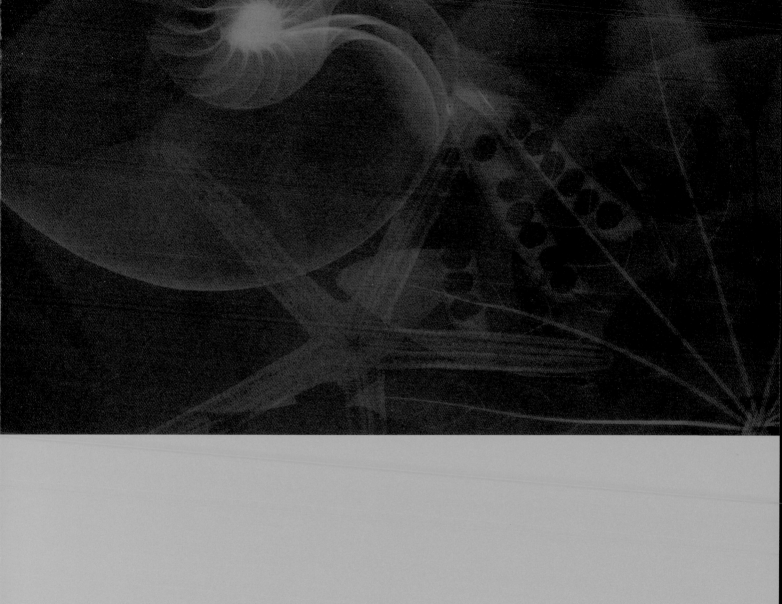

Index

Index

Page numbers for definitions are shown in **bold**. Page numbers for figures and tables are shown in *italic*.